FLORENCE

THE (

Ponte V
Dating b
gamut c
buskers

Corrido
Built in
Grand D
connect
T 055 29

Museo (
A synap
objects
such as
Piazza d

Galleri
Vasari's
of the w
Piazzale

Palazzo
Ignore t
Il Crona
See p01

Basilica
The forr
Donatel
See p00

Museo (
Highligh
Renaiss
Bacchus
See p00

Duomo
Still dominating the skyline, the basilica's colossal dome was designed by Brunelleschi.
See p010

INTRODUCTION

THE CHANGING FACE OF THE URBAN SCENE

The Renaissance was about to eat itself, but Florence fought back. It's in the throes of a civic renaissance. Faced with an annual deluge of 12 million tourists (that's 32 for every local) vying for a glimpse of Giotto and Michelangelo's genius, as well as countless palazzi, churches and museums, it rethought its infrastructure to counter the interminable queues and gridlocked pavements. Many *cittadini* still fear their home is going the way of Venice and are demanding more – and in 2017, mayor Dario Nardella ordered historic sites be hosed down to keep picnickers at bay. However, the embryonic tram network is at last spreading its tendrils, the orange wheels of dockless Mobikes are visible around town, and the Firenzecard allows subscribers to skip the lines. The city now has the musical colossus (see p014) that it deserves, and business incentives have inspired a crop of high-end retailers, bars and restaurants in the *centro storico*. Plus, the staggering surfeit of cultural riches means you can always find wonders a few blocks away from the crowds.

But we'd advise you visit between October and March to avoid the sweltering summers altogether, and swerve the bloated centre as much as you can, instead distributing your largesse among the ateliers, artists' studios and locals' bars south of the river – on the 'other side' – in Oltrarno. Here, contemporary galleries laid down a marker and, more recently, a slew of stylish venues has opened, alongside the characterful workshops and high-quality *trattorie*.

ESSENTIAL INFO

FACTS, FIGURES AND USEFUL ADDRESSES

TOURIST OFFICE
Via Camillo Cavour 1
T 055 290 832
www.firenzeturismo.it

TRANSPORT
Airport transfer to city centre
A bus shuttle service runs every half hour between 5.30am and 12.30am. Transit time is 20 minutes
Car hire
Hertz
Via del Sansovino 53
T 055 713 5172
Taxis
It Taxi
www.4390.it/en.it-taxi-app
So.Co.Ta
T 055 4242
Cabs cannot be hailed in the street but there are numerous ranks in the centre
Firenzecard museum pass
www.firenzecard.it

EMERGENCY SERVICES
Emergencies
T 112
24-hour pharmacy
Farmacia Comunale Santa Maria Novella
Stazione Santa Maria Novella
T 055 264 6371

CONSULATES
British Consulate General
Via San Paolo 7
Milan
T 02 723 001
www.gov.uk/world/italy
US Consulate
Lungarno Vespucci 38
T 055 266 951
it.usembassy.gov

POSTAL SERVICES
Post office
Via Pellicceria 3
Shipping
Mail Boxes Etc
Via della Scala 13
T 055 268 173

BOOKS
The Divine Comedy by Dante Alighieri (Oxford World's Classics)
Florence: The Biography of a City by Christopher Hibbert (Penguin)
A Room With a View by EM Forster (Penguin Classics)
Super Superstudio by Andreas Angelidakis, Vittorio Pizzigoni and Valter Scelsi (Silvana Editoriale)

WEBSITES
Art
www.strozzina.org/en
Newspaper
www.theflorentine.net

EVENTS
Florence Biennale
www.florencebiennale.org/en
Florence Design Week
www.florencedesignweek.com

COST OF LIVING
Taxi from Vespucci Airport to city centre
€23
Cappuccino
€2
Packet of cigarettes
€5
Daily newspaper
€1.50
Bottle of champagne
€46

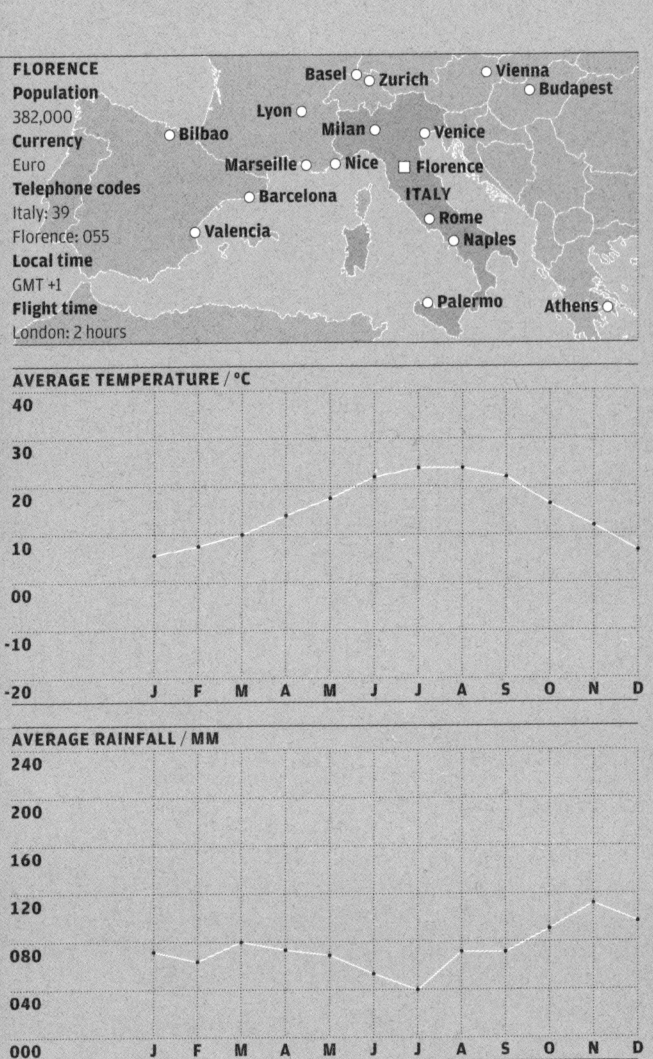
FLORENCE
Population
382,000
Currency
Euro
Telephone codes
Italy: 39
Florence: 055
Local time
GMT +1
Flight time
London: 2 hours
Basel
Zurich
Vienna
Budapest
Lyon
Bilbao
Milan
Venice
Marseille
Nice
Florence
Barcelona
ITALY
Rome
Valencia
Naples
Palermo
Athens
AVERAGE TEMPERATURE / °C
40
30
20
10
00
-10
-20
J F M A M J J A S O N D
AVERAGE RAINFALL / MM
240
200
160
120
080
040
000
J F M A M J J A S O N D

NEIGHBOURHOODS

THE AREAS YOU NEED TO KNOW AND WHY

To help you navigate the city, we've chosen the most interesting districts (see below and the map inside the back cover) and colour-coded our featured venues, according to their location; those venues that are outside these areas are not coloured.

SANTA MARIA NOVELLA

A stealthy upgrade has revamped Piazza Santa Maria Novella and etched a tramline alongside the rationalist station (see p076), sprucing up landscaping to boot. Providing the Renaissance firepower are the frescoes displayed in Cappella dei Magi (Via Cavour 3, T 055 276 0340) and the baroque Chiesa di Ognissanti (Borgo Ognissanti 42, T 055 239 8700). The leafy boulevards towards the Arno host a coterie of solid hotels such as Kraft (Via Solferino 2, T 055 284 273).

SAN MARCO

Bolstering this quarter's green lung credentials is the city's first community garden, Orti Dipinti (Borgo Pinti 76). It's a boho counterpoint to Giardino di Palazzo Capponi (Via Gino Capponi 26) and Giardino della Gherardesca within the Four Seasons (Borgo Pinti 99, T 055 26 261). The cultural draws are the Opificio delle Pietre Dure Museum (Via degli Alfani 78, T 055 26 511) and Galleria dell'Accademia (see p024).

CAMPO DI MARTE

The sporting district offers top-quality football clashes at the glorious 1930s Stadio Artemio Franchi (see p013), the home ground of ACF Fiorentina, as well as more egalitarian five-a-side kickabouts and exercise classes at Atletica Firenze Marathon (Viale Manfredo Fanti 2, T 055 553 2982). Head south to discover one of Florence's modern architectural triumphs, the avant-garde Sacro Cuore (see p072).

OLTRARNO

This fast-gentrifying swathe south of the river is the roost for creative enterprise including late-night bars (see p032) and gig venues like NOF (Borgo San Frediano 17, T 333 614 5376) – city residents flee here to avoid the stampedes in Disneyland Florence. A strong artisan spirit endures in ateliers such as Sartoria Vestrucci (Via Maggio 58, T 055 289 297). And make a beeline for Brancacci's chapel in Chiesa Santa Maria del Carmine (see p024).

SANTA CROCE

Natives have mustered a feisty rearguard action here. Drop by for a pocket-friendly lunch at Trattoria da Rocco (Piazza Ghiberti, T 339 838 4555), coffee at Ditta Artigianale (see p047) and the foodie empire of Fabio Picchi (see p040). Even the Renaissance attractions are fairly unstressful, including the rambling Basilica di Santa Croce (see p073) and the Sinagoga e Museo Ebraico (Via Luigi Carlo Farini 6, T 055 234 6654).

SAN GIOVANNI

Shoals of somnambulant tourists swim across the heart of the *centro storico* so get up with the lark to enjoy a crowd-free Duomo (see p010) or Loggia dei Lanzi (Piazza della Signoria), famous for its al fresco Cellini and Giambologna marble statues, and book ahead for the Galleria degli Uffizi (see p009). Meanwhile, Via de' Tornabuoni retains its sheen with a gamut of high-end jewellers and fashion stores.

LANDMARKS

THE SHAPE OF THE CITY SKYLINE

Florence's skyline has changed very little in 600 years. Brunelleschi's stately crown for the Duomo (overleaf) has lorded it over the city since the 15th century, while palazzi such as the Medici's dazzling inaugural seat, Palazzo Medici Riccardi (Via Camillo Cavour 3), continue to steal the limelight, unless they are cloaked as part of an ongoing restoration programme. For anything this side of 1900, you will have to make a pilgrimage north-west, to the fascist-era Stazione Santa Maria Novella (see p076), and the contemporary Palazzo di Giustizia (see p078) and Maggio Musicale (see p014).

To get the measure of Florence, head to Piazzale Michelangelo. From here you will see the Arno scythe through the world's finest collection of Renaissance architecture. On the north side of the river, the medieval crush can be overwhelming: Museo del Bargello (Via del Proconsolo 4, T 055 238 8606) and the Galleria degli Uffizi (Piazzale degli Uffizi 6, T 055 294 883) stand out, and ecclesiastical heavyweights such as Basilica di Santa Croce (see p073) to the east, and Basilica di San Lorenzo (Piazza San Lorenzo 9, T 055 216 634) to the north, on the site of the city's original cathedral, dwarf all that surrounds them. By contrast, the south bank has more room to breathe. Beyond Palazzo Pitti (Piazza Pitti 1, T 055 294 883) is the Giardino di Boboli (see p066) and Via di San Leonardo, a lane lined with villas, one of which was inhabited by Tchaikovsky.

For full addresses, see Resources.

Duomo

The real point of Florence's cathedral is its sheer, fear-of-God bulk, which seems to stretch Piazza del Duomo at the seams. Stand as far back as you can to take in Arnolfo di Cambio's 13th-century marble-clad marvel, the engineering genius of Filippo Brunelleschi's double-shelled cupola, Giotto's belltower and Emilio De Fabris' 1887 neo-Gothic facade. Mercifully, a 2016 proposition by McDonald's to open in the square was flatly refused. Instead, investment was pumped into a restoration of the church and an upgrade of Museo dell'Opera del Duomo, now a refuge for 750 medieval and Renaissance reliefs and statues wrought by Lorenzo Ghiberti, Donatello et al that previously adorned nearby buildings. Book ahead in order to clamber the 463 steps to the dome, which is still the city's tallest structure at 112m. *Piazza del Duomo 17, T 055 230 2885, www.museumflorence.com*

Palazzo Vecchio

Impossible to miss because of its soaring 94m-high belltower, this fortified palazzo, completed in 1314, is a spiky reminder of Florence's brief stint as Italy's capital; the parliament was based here from 1865 to 1871. Designed by Arnolfo di Cambio to house the city's priors, it was tinkered with by Michelozzo, Vasari and Buontalenti in the following three centuries, resulting in a rather lopsided affair. It's a reference point for all those souls tramping from the Duomo (see p010) to the Uffizi (see p009), but to look no further than the replica of Michelangelo's *David* out front would be a mistake. Inside are wonders including the glittering Salone dei Cinquecento, and Francesco I's studio, with secret cabinets used to guard his scientific breakthroughs. *Piazza della Signoria, T 055 276 8325, www.museicivicifiorentini.comune.fi.it/en*

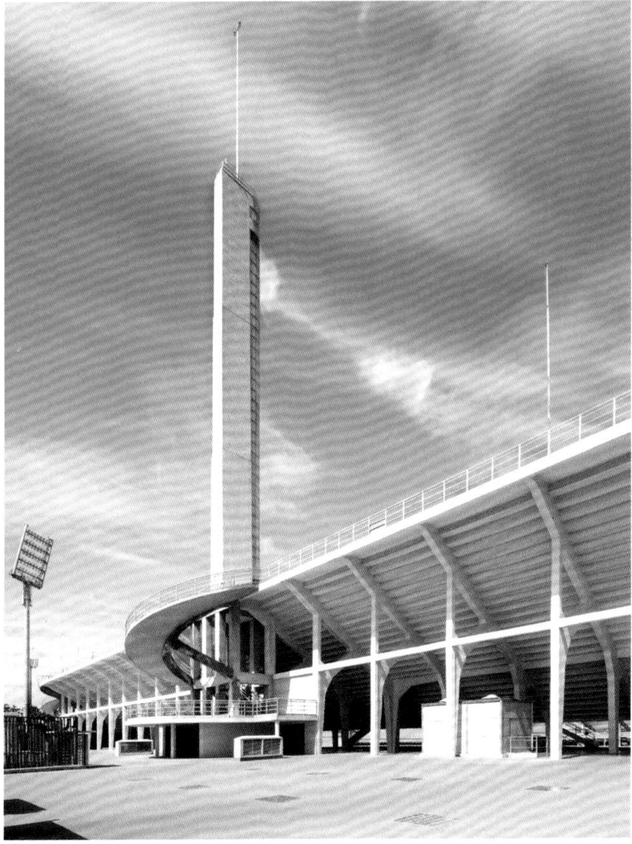

Stadio Artemio Franchi

ACF Fiorentina's home ground, completed in 1931, bears all the bombastic symmetry and quake-in-your-boots magnitude of Mussolini-era projects. Designed by Pier Luigi Nervi and Alessandro Giuntoli, it's a graceful symphony in reinforced concrete, with helical staircases and neoclassical columns, flagged by a strident 70m tower. A spruce-up for the 1990 FIFA World Cup removed an athletics track to increase the seating capacity to 43,000. However, with fans and officials of the opinion that the venue has become a hindrance to the club's footballing fortunes (most of its rivals have upgraded facilities), its future depends on the progress of a masterplan for a purpose-built stadium as part of the regeneration of an entire suburb out near the airport.
Viale Manfredo Fanti 4, T 055 503 011, en.violachannel.tv

Maggio Musicale Fiorentino

Architects ABDR's opera house and concert hall opened in 2011 and is Florence's only truly contemporary civic blockbuster. The geometry and competing angles play with perspective so that the main Kerlite-clad rhomboid resembles a glacier slipping into the ocean. It's flanked by wide staircases that lead up to the masterstroke – a huge tiered amphitheatre, Cavea, on the roof, which stages performances under the Tuscan moon on summer evenings. The complex is crowned by a darker volume that houses rehearsal rooms and offices, and all is beautifully illuminated at night. If you don't have time to catch a show, at least come to admire the building, and then pop into the beer garden at Buonerìa (T 055 365 500) nearby for cocktails and DJ sets.
Piazzale Vittorio Gui 1, T 055 277 9309, www.operadifirenze.it

HOTELS

WHERE TO STAY AND WHICH ROOMS TO BOOK

A more demanding visitor has prompted this traditional city to up its game, and many of its hotels have added immersive experiences. The Lungarno Group (see p020) marshals 'lifestyle teams' to run Vespa trips, and Relais Santa Croce (Via Ghibellina 87, T 055 234 2230) organises perfume tours – its very Florentine 18th-century frescoes, fireplaces and staircases no longer enough of a draw on their own. Firenze Number Nine (Via dei Conti 9, T 055 293 777) opened as a wellness retreat that champions Arya rebirthing and detox massages. And Olga Polizzi's upgrade of the Savoy (Piazza della Repubblica 7, T 055 27 351) mixes C&C Milano fabrics, B&B chairs and Cassina 'Cicognino' coffee tables with the usual swathes of polished marble and exquisitely carved furniture. A number of these establishments collaborated to launch Firenze Yes Please, an online guide featuring city insiders and below-the-radar events.

There are some truly original offerings. The boho Le Tre Stanze (Via dell'Oriuolo 43, T 329 212 8756) is the meditative retreat of sculptor Patrick John-Steiner, complete with walled garden, just moments from the Duomo, and Casa Schlatter (Viale dei Mille 14, T 347 118 0215) is the 19th-century atelier of Swiss painter Carlo Adolfo Schlatter, and full of his work. Two of the most accomplished ventures (opposite) are run by Betty Soldi, and if you're harbouring Grand Tour fantasies, these are the only places to lay your trunk.

For full addresses and room rates, see Resources.

SoprArno Suites

Calligrapher Betty Soldi, partner Matteo Perduca and architect Francesco Maestrelli have conceived two of Florence's most unique properties, both in 16th-century palazzos in Oltrarno, the city's Left Bank. Opened in 2014 around the corner from bar-laden Piazza San Spirito, SoprArno is the more urbane. Here, the eclectic decor features vintage finds and classic pieces. All of the 13 suites are different and often themed – for instance, one is inspired by typography, while Deluxe 26 (above) is portrayed as a 'stylish gentleman's room'. Sister property AdAstra (T 055 075 0602) was unveiled a year later, and is more of an ancestral retreat, with its grand staircase and painted ceilings, and a perfect setting overlooking the lovely Giardino Torrigiani. *Via Maggio 35, T 055 046 8719, www.soprarnosuites.com/en*

Il Salviatino

When *centro storico* thermometers nudge 30 degrees centigrade, it's time to head out to this 15th-century *nobili* villa, just 15 minutes north-west of town among the sweet air of the Fiesole hills. Il Salviatino has always been better out than in, with multi-level formal gardens and panoramic city vistas outclassing the slightly hollow baronial-hall-style common areas. However, Alessandra and Luca Rovati, owners since 2016, have been injecting brightness and warmth. Of the 44 rooms, opt for the Affresco Suite (pictured), with its 19th-century Bruschi fresco. Spend your days floating in the tiered pool, surrounded by restorative green and chirping cicadas, and enjoying mod-meets-trad cuisine on the terrace.
Via del Salviatino 21, T 055 904 1111, www.salviatino.com

Portrait

This sleek riverside hideaway is the most fashionable of the four upmarket hotels in the group run by Leonardo Ferragamo (son of Salvatore), despite the refurb of the more classic Lungarno (T 055 2726 4000) in 2017. Architect and interior designer Michele Bönan has applied his trademark minimalism across all 37 rooms – every one a suite rendered in muted greys and pure white lines, punctuated with witty touches such as gilded pineapples. *La Dolce Vita*-era photos of Audrey Hepburn, Roberto Capucci and Ferragamo Senior adorn the walls, bathrooms are clad in *pietra toscana*, and discreet kitchenettes are equipped with coffee machines and hotplates. The Ponte Vecchio Suite (above) terrace has views of the iconic bridge.
Lungarno degli Acciaiuoli 4, T 055 2726 8000, www.lungarnocollection.com

JK Place

While sticking to a 'gentleman's townhouse' template, this 2003 institution is evolving to retain its boutique crown. A champagne bar opened in 2015 and the lounge sports photography by Dario Garofalo. There are now own-brand cashmere blankets and fragrances, wi-fi dongles for guests' use around town, and the Penthouse has a tub overlooking the Duomo. The biggest change is the aspect: the hotel helped to finance the 2012 upgrade of Piazza Santa Maria Novella and, to benefit further, has since added a dining terrace out front. The canvas is classical – Charles XVI fireplaces (lobby, above) and *pietra serena* – but the decoration displays flashes of eccentricity like zebra-skin ottomans, and the breakfast room is pure English country house.
Piazza Santa Maria Novella 7,
T 055 264 5181, www.jkplace.com/en

Riva Lofts

Architect Claudio Nardi has managed to conjure up a vibe that's a cross between a farmhouse and a slick city apartment block out of an artisan workshop on the Arno's south bank. A sitting room features an open fire under ancient brick vaults, and the furniture selection encompasses Ico Parisi armchairs, 1950s and 1960s Italian and Nordic tables and chairs, Flos' 'Taccia' lighting, and original pieces by Nardi. The 10 suites are accented in soft grey and incorporate clever touches such as concealed hobs and sinks. Bag Studio Seven, which opens onto the garden and pool (above), or the Loft Studio (opposite), with its four-poster bed and terrace. Riva encourages outdoor pursuits, such as bike rides in Parco delle Cascine, past Maggio Musicale (see p014), across the river. The tram zips you to the centre in six minutes.
Via Baccio Bandinelli 98, T 055 713 0272, www.rivalofts.com/en

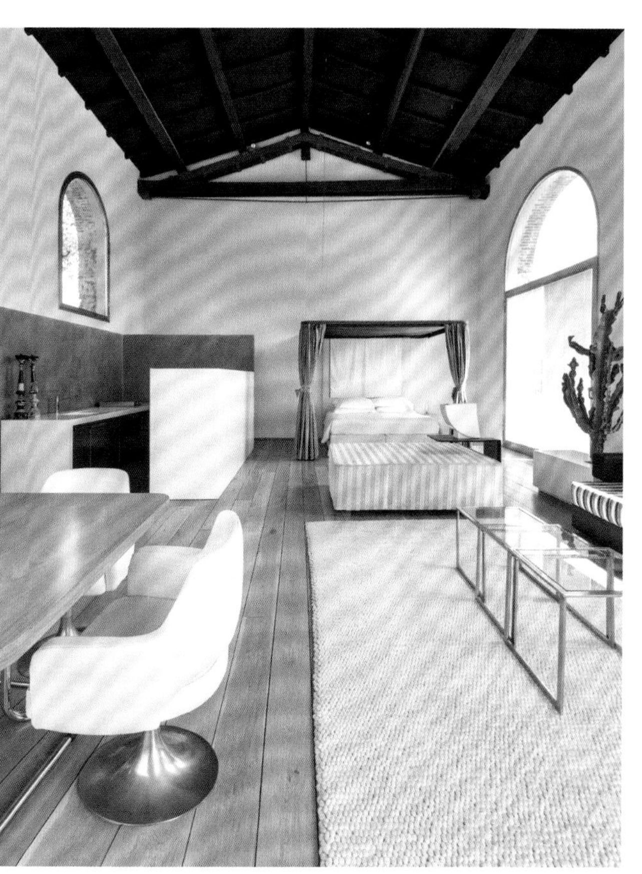

24 HOURS

SEE THE BEST OF THE CITY IN JUST ONE DAY

It's easy to succumb to antiquity fatigue here, so dilute the wonders of the Renaissance with contemporary culture and regular pitstops at multitasking venues like Ditta Artigianale (see p047). If you are dead set on bagging the Duomo (see p010), Michelangelo's *Schiavi* at Galleria dell'Accademia (Via Ricasoli 58-60, T 055 294 883) and Botticelli's *Birth of Venus* at the Uffizi (see p009), book ahead so as not to drown in a tsunami of tourists, or buy a Firenzecard, which gives you access to 72 museums in 72 hours (good luck with that).

The real trick is to seek out the sublime works in lesser-known sites, in particular Museo del Bargello (see p009); the spectacular frescoes by Masolino, Masaccio and Lippi at the Brancacci Chapel in Chiesa Santa Maria del Carmine (Piazza del Carmine 14, T 055 238 2195); and Andrea del Sarto's extraordinary *Last Supper* in the Cenacolo (Via di San Salvi 16, T 055 238 8603). Intersperse this with the neoteric highlights, of which there are surprisingly many, from Museo Novecento (opposite) to Eduardo Secci (see p063).

By the end of the day, you'll have earned a meal fit for nobility at Gurdulù (see p031), or Cuculia (Via dei Serragli 3, T 055 277 6205), which is a vegan and vegetarian delight, and also serves biodynamic wines and a mean Sunday brunch. In the summer, pop-up beach Easy Living (Piazza Giuseppe Poggi, T 055 234 1112) provides a welcome breather, offering cocktails and DJ sets next to the Arno.

For full addresses, see Resources.

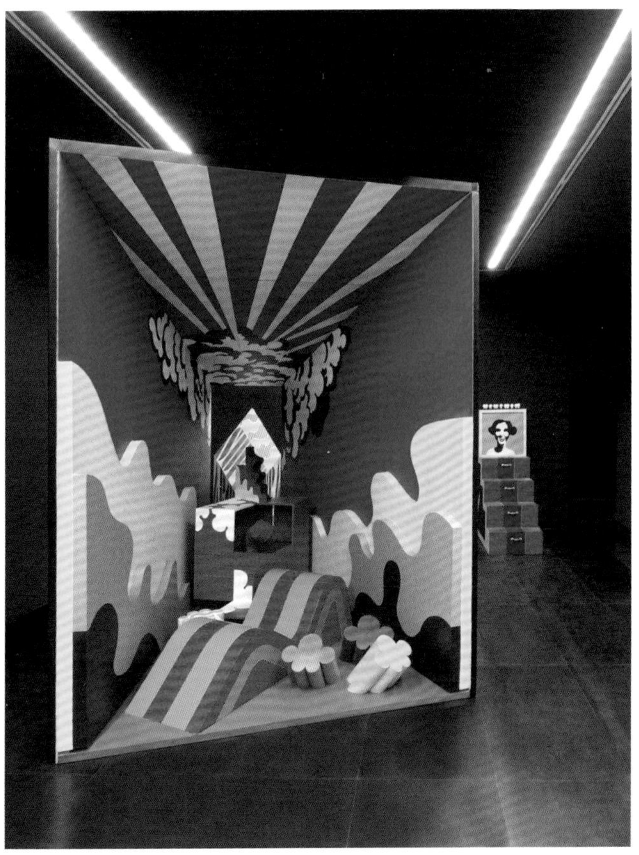

10.30 Museo Novecento

Set within a 13th-century hospital complex, this superlative museum gives an overview of 100 years of Italian art and culture by investigating a series of select movements and periods. The 300 or so works take you backwards (unfathomably) from the 1990s to the early 20th century. Highlights are the focus on the surreal counterculture happenings at the city's Schema gallery, non-profit experimental space Zona and video production centre Art/Tapes/22 from 1973 to 1976; and a study of Archizoom and Superstudio's Superarchitettura concept (above), a cross-pollination of design, the visual arts, architecture, music and mass communication that took hold in the 1960s. Head to the top-floor cinema for the finale: a mash-up of cuts from Florentine films.
Piazza Santa Maria Novella 10,
T 055 286 132, www.museonovecento.it

13.00 La Ménagère

In this multipurpose venue, you can pick up flowers from Artemisia, browse tableware and design objects, and kick back in the café or restaurant (above); there's even a downstairs lounge that hosts live jazz on Thursdays to Sundays. It was the city's first homewares store, opened in 1896, and the brickwork, crumbling plaster and vaults are original. Q-Bic's reimagining created a series of connected areas, decorated with reclaimed and bespoke furniture, Karmen lighting, geometric tiling (opposite) and hanging plants. The all-day menu features Tuscan classics like *guancia di manzo* (beef cheek), *coniglio in porchetta alla cacciatora* (roast rabbit) and vin santo mousse, and cocktails include the Bourbon & Brunch (mixed with bacon, tomato juice and lime). *Via dè Ginori 8, T 055 075 0600, www.lamenagere.it*

ITALY
ITALY
ITALY

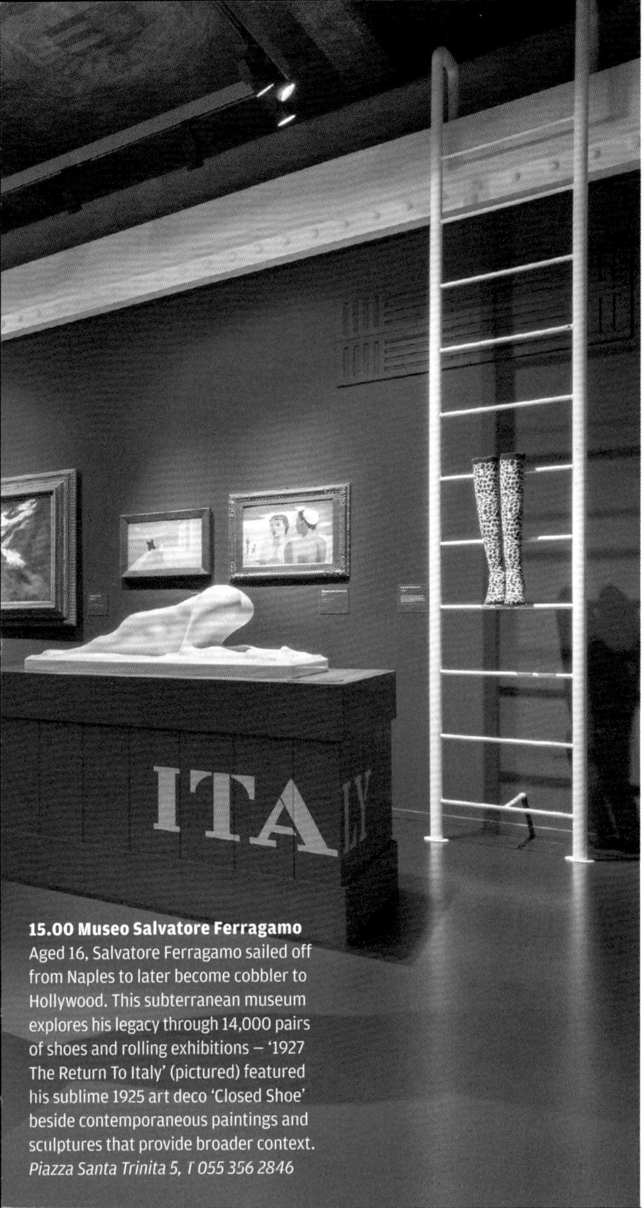

15.00 Museo Salvatore Ferragamo
Aged 16, Salvatore Ferragamo sailed off from Naples to later become cobbler to Hollywood. This subterranean museum explores his legacy through 14,000 pairs of shoes and rolling exhibitions – '1927 The Return To Italy' (pictured) featured his sublime 1925 art deco 'Closed Shoe' beside contemporaneous paintings and sculptures that provide broader context.
Piazza Santa Trinita 5, T 055 356 2846

18.00 Soulspace

Zelal Elbistan's spa and beauty centre, just a few paces east of the Duomo (see p010), is a nerve-soothing bolthole fashioned out of an 18th-century palazzo by architects Stefano Mannucci and Lorenzo Leoncini. The packages are a good option, offering combos of pool, steam room, massage and face and body sessions to suit your mood, and a wide range of treatments includes Tibetan sand and hot-stone massages. The real boon, though, is the centre's interiors, under the original high, vaulted ceilings, from the putty-grey reception area to the shimmering jade pool (above) and marble-clad Turkish hammam (Elbistan grew up in Istanbul). And if you fear you will never surface from your reverie, try a few sharp intakes of air in the pretty decked garden.
Via Sant'Egidio 12, T 055 200 1794,
www.soulspace.it

21.00 Gurdulù

Tucked down a side street, Gurdulù offers high-end dining and slick cocktails. For its 2015 launch, Studio Tricot gave it a moody vibe, with battered and bare wood floors, swirling-cloud chiaroscuro wall coverings, dark blue hues and spotlights, candle-like wall sconces and globe pendants, while Antonio Sciacca's symbolist Madonna and anatomical wooden hearts by Moradi Il Sedicente provide Gothic touches. There's also a lovely courtyard for summer. Kick off with a Stone Martini, a concoction of Ligurian beach pebbles, gin and vermouth, before sampling chef Gabriele Andreoni's finely crafted dishes, like yellowtail with leek, artichokes, chestnuts and a green apple reduction. The sommelier will advise on the 250-plus wines. Closed Mondays.
Via delle Caldaie 12, T 055 282 223, www.gurdulu.com

URBAN LIFE

CAFÉS, RESTAURANTS, BARS AND NIGHTCLUBS

The city's dining scene is buoyant. Mayor Dario Nardella, cementing predecessor Matteo Renzi's 'can do' pluck, is energising the sector by cracking down on kebab shops, fronting up to McDonald's and decreeing that the menus of new eateries focus on Tuscan produce. La Ménagère (see p026) and Foody Farm (see p038) are blowing away cobwebs in the *centro storico* with traceable ingredients and all-day kitchens. Fabio Picchi is bolstering his empire (see p040), which is headed up by Cibrèo (Via del Verrocchio 8, T 055 234 1100). Those still with expense accounts should book a table at Cantinetta Antinori (Piazza Antinori 3, T 055 292 234) or the triple-Michelin-starred Enoteca Pinchiorri (Via Ghibellina 87, T 055 242 757).

In Oltrarno, #Raw (see p034) and Italian Tapas (see p043) rip up the rulebook altogether with vegan shots and self-service, and bars such as MAD Souls & Spirits (Borgo San Frediano 36, T 055 627 1621) and speakeasy Rasputin (Borgo Tegolaio 21, T 055 280 399) bring a global vibe. Of course, the classic venues remain. The *petti di pollo al burro* (buttered chicken breasts) at 1869 Trattoria Sostanza (Via del Porcellana 25, T 055 212 691) is a must, as is a slab of *bistecca* at Buca Lapi (Via del Trebbio 1, T 055 213 768). Florence isn't big on clubs, but you can mix views with cocktails in summer at Flò (Piazzale Michelangelo 84, T 055 650 791), and hit the floor year round at revamped classic Yab (Via dei Sassetti 5, T 055 215 160).
For full addresses, see Resources.

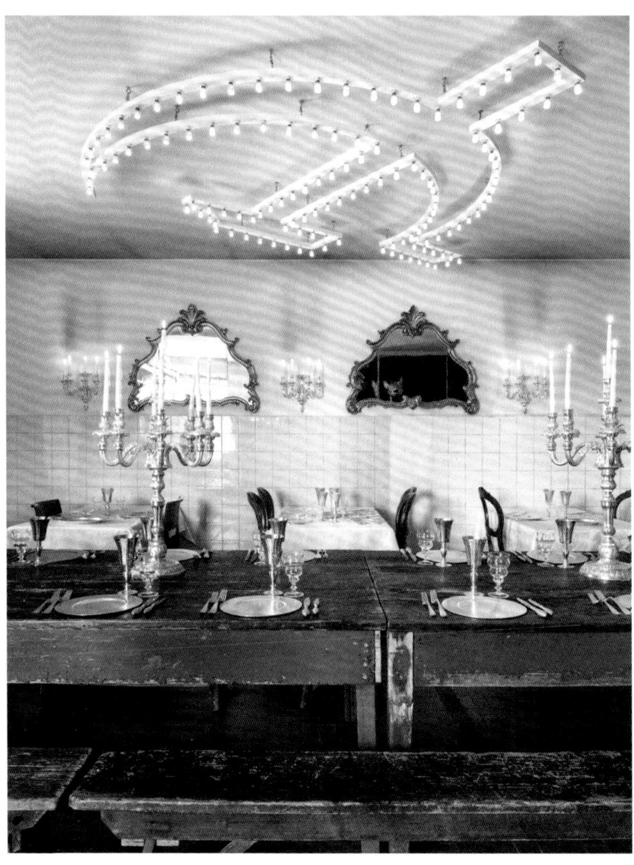

Pampaloni

Located in Gianfranco Pampaloni's working silversmith's, this restaurant is worth the 15-minute cab ride for its artisan setting and ribald political critique as much as the Sicilian fare. Pick up a welcome drink in the showroom, and admire creations such as an outsized €20,000 chess set, a tiny egg timer given to Oscar winners in 2002 to curtail rambling speeches, and hidden posters sending up Kim Jong-un and other megalomaniacs. Head past the clunking 1930s to 1950s machinery to the dining room on the first floor, illuminated by candelabra and a lightbulb hammer and sickle. Hits of the menu are the buffalo mozzarella ravioli with pistachio, breaded swordfish steak, and cassata with ricotta cheese and candied fruit. Dinner only.
Via del Gelsomino 99, T 347 514 5468, restaurant.pampaloni.com

#Raw

Manfredi Mangris and Caroline Lundgren's vegan, organic, gluten-free café has been attracting healthy-eaters in droves since 2016. There are few other places in town where you can find raw cacao coldpress nutmilk, or shots of wheatgrass, spirulina and aloe vera, while there are also wraps, salads (try the *alga* nori), cakes and pizza, a long list of fruit smoothies and delicious gelati. You feel cleansed as soon as you enter the dinky two-part space behind a palm-fringed street terrace. Lundgren has infused a meditative ambience, with lo-fi compressed-board tables, pillows for back rests, slender silver birch trunks and suspended water-filled glass balls, each sporting a green sprig. Continue the body-conscious regime around the corner at Italia Power Yoga (T 349 534 0565).
Via Sant'Agostino 11, T 055 219 379

La Cucina di Pescepane

Launched in 2015 with little more than an Apé truck, a fryer and a mean line in anchovies, this street-food outfit weighed anchor close to Sant'Ambrogio market in 2017, offering keenly priced plates to eat in or take away. Try the signature *gran fritto misto* of calamari and giant prawn, the *trippa di mare* (a squid-based riff on the local obsession with tripe), crostini, tuna tartare or the take on cod and chips. Naturally leavened Tuscan bread, supplied by nearby Panificio Elleci (T 055 242 811) is rightly ubiquitous. Takk Design Studio has conjured a subtle maritime mood via turquoise walls, 1950s chairs and Sardinian basket traps repurposed as lampshades. Finish with the Zuccotto Carapina, an icy *bombe* of ricotta in feather-light sponge. *Via Giosuè Carducci 15, T 055 234 4397, www.pescepane.it*

Libreria Brac

Hugely popular at weekends, Libreria Brac was established by Sandro Sandri Olmo and Melisa Di Nardo. It's an art bookshop, veggie and vegan restaurant, and bar and event space, hosting wine tastings, photo exhibitions and film screenings. Through the back, in the glass-walled eaterie, you can tuck into pear carpaccio, spaghettini with tomato and basil, Sardinian flatbread and delicious salads, such as kale, mustard, raisin and apple. A courtyard features an aerial forest of 5,000 hanging fabric strips created by architects Deferrari+Modesti in conjunction with Valentina Muscedra and Sergio Leone. If it happens to be free, repair to the cosy enclave (opposite), with a gramophone player and rack of *Mousse* magazines, for a low-key hour or two.
Via dei Vagellai 18, T 055 094 4877, www.libreriabrac.net

Foody Farm

Owner Pierluigi Bizzarri is an advocate of a return to 100 per cent Tuscan ingredients traceable to farm and field at this venture. And since it opened in 2017, locals have been going wild for top-notch *soprassata* sausage from Fattoria Il Colle, seared beef from Maremma, and pomegranate wheat ale from Prato brewery Canediguerra. Bizzarri's company Bizionaire, which also runs Fishing Lab (see p048), has gone for a farmhouse vibe here, with reclaimed wood panelling, mismatched pendant lamps, patchwork banquette seating and a 'living wall' of potted plants. Dishes are equally consciously crafted, offered in categories such as 'street foody' and 'raw foody', and served as sliders, or on metal shovels and in compartmentalised wooden trays.
Corso dei Tintori 10, T 055 242 327,
www.foodyfarm.it

Ora d'Aria

Chef Marco Stabile has built his reputation on a culinary style that approaches art. He developed his *cucina toscana rivisitata*, in which he combines staples like pigeon with high-end delicacies, through stints at some of Italy's top restaurants, including Osteria di Passignano (T 055 807 1278), just south of Florence in Chianti country (see p100). Here, he excels in dishes such as low-temperature-cooked suckling pig with mushroom sauce and kale kimchi; risotto with bitter herb liquor; and ginger and roasted bell-pepper ice cream. The interiors, by Mariella Corsi of Prato firm Archbcstudio, are a graceful exposition in white and grey, with parquet floors and backlit shelves showcasing vintages from quality producers like Ornellaia and Gaja. *Via dei Georgofili 11, T 055 200 1699, www.oradariaristorante.com*

###Ciblèo Tortelli e Ravioli

Celeb chef Fabio Picchi brought his local cuisine to the Far East by opening in Japan in 1988, and in 2017 he turned the tables, now serving up Tuscan-Oriental fusions, such as spicy samosa cannoli and sesame-oil-anointed ravioli, on his native patch of Sant'Ambrogio. Ciblèo is installed in a tiny triangle that was once a button atelier and has a vaulted brick ceiling, recycled wood shutters, framed Japanese script and a painting of Il Ponte Vecchio by Picchi's son Giulio. It can accommodate just 18 diners, with eight seats at the counter that fronts the action-packed kitchen, managed by Korean Minjoo Heo, plus a couple of tables outside. Order the taster menu to sample more than 20 delicate, innovative small plates, from dim sum to broths, and do try the toffee-infused Wa Jukusei Nama sake. Dinner only. Closed Sunday and Monday.
Via del Verrocchio 2, T 055 247 7881,
www.cibreo.com/en

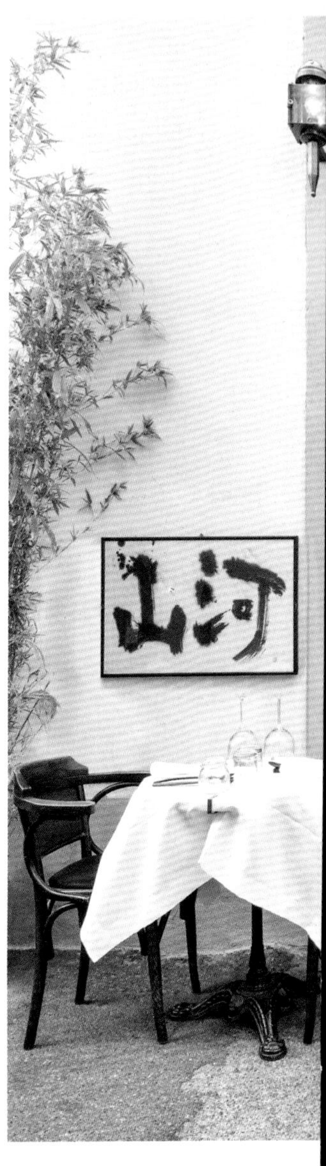

TORTELLI E RAVIOLI

Essenziale

In a barn-like venue under a wood-beam roof, chef Simone Cipriani, and sommelier Federico Fametti and team, puncture the pretentiousness of high-end dining with wallet-friendly tasting dishes and an open preparation area on the mezzanine. The interior, by Moreno Vannini and Cipriani, is spartan yet spirited: sleek tables sport concealed cutlery drawers and recycled rubber tops, and landmarks are rendered convex in Martini Dini's 'Spoon' photos. Order a glass of Castello di Meleto Chianti Classico to accompany the excellent four-course menu, which might offer up juicy slivers of octopus with onion, cucumber and basil; rabbit tagliatelle; pork belly with artichokes; and *fior d'evo* (meringue, ice cream and olive-oil summer pudding). *Piazza di Cestello 3, T 055 247 6956, www.essenziale.me*

Italian Tapas

Brothers Marco and Matteo Laporta have taken an inventive approach at their 2016 restaurant and cocktail bar. In the interior, architects Nemogruppo and Fattorini Lab have melded chic and rustic, with bespoke spruce and beech tables, a bar and walls built up from layers of reclaimed wood, and lighting fashioned out of terracotta pots by Cosmotre; there is also a shady courtyard. The fare is even more creative. An antipasti, primi and secondi line-up is eschewed in favour of tapas-style dishes, perhaps mussel-topped risotto, marinated octopus, or beef-liver skewers. The drinks include gazpacho cocktails and ginger and berry antioxidant shots. Kick off with the signature Porretta Mule cocktail, which is mixed with vodka, lime and raspberry jam.
Via Sant'Agostino 11, T 055 098 2738, www.italiantapas.it

Gosh

Lebanese brothers Alexander and Matteo Vartivarian have created one of the city's hippest bars on a shoestring budget and with a magpie's eye for interiors. Founded in 2017, the appropriately named Gosh is festooned with flamingo damask found in the Marais, with a plastic chandelier and lights rescued from a bombed-out hotel in Aleppo, handmade tables from Beirut and 1950s chairs made in the GDR. The counter is a spirited mash-up too, amalgamating slabs of tea rose and Carrara off-white marble. The barrier-vaulting atmosphere draws Fiorentini of all ages until the small hours at weekends; there's also live funk, soul and jazz on Thursdays after 10pm. Try the feisty Été Indien cocktail, which is made with rum, lime and grapefruit juice, almond syrup and Elemakule Tiki Bitters.
Via di Santo Spirito 46, T 055 046 9048

Zeb

Once just a local food store, Zeb morphed into a futuristic diner and upscale deli in 2007. Run by mother and son Giuseppina Culella and Alberto Navari, the tiny eaterie has a long single counter around which diners perch on 15 faux-leather bar stools. The season-driven menu is mostly Tuscan, such as pappardelle with wild-boar ragu or the springtime favourite of pecorino-and-ricotta-filled ravioli with pear sauce, and *secondi piatti* of *peposo* (beef in red wine and peppercorns) or rabbit loin stuffed with liver, garlic, herbs and cheese. If it's available, try the tangy *schiacciata con l'uva* – a flat, oven-baked cake with grapes and aniseed – and take home staples such as salami finocchiona, made with fennel seeds. Note it keeps odd opening hours.
Via San Miniato 2, T 055 234 2864, www.zebgastronomia.com

Ditta Artigianale

Occupying a ground floor and mezzanine of a Giovanni Michelucci (see p074) building finished in 1958, café/bar Ditta Artigianale pays homage to the era. It opened in 2016 after a refurbishment by Q-Bic brothers Luca and Marco Baldini, also responsible for La Ménagère (see p026). Here, they chose polished concrete, mosaic tiles and midcentury-style geometric panelling, and installed Gianfranco Frattini chairs and own-design pieces, all centred around a retro Marzocco espresso machine. This is the second offering from three-time Italian barista champion Francesco Sanapo – the original in Santa Croce (T 055 274 1541) is more studenty. Order a matcha latte and a Chianina beef tartare. Or visit after 6pm, when the gin bar unleashes its 150 labels. *Via Dello Sprone 5, T 055 045 7163, www.dittaartigianale.it*

Fishing Lab Alle Murate

Pierluigi Bizzarri's buzzy restaurant moved into Palazzo dell'Arte dei Giudici e Notai in 2016, and provides a history lesson along with a fine fish supper. The ceiling is the canvas for 14th-century frescoes, including restored portraits of Dante and Giovanni Boccaccio, and you can spy an excavated 1st-century wool-dying room through a glass floor. And although traditionalists will baulk at the thought of eating fish in Florence when the coast is a 90-minute drive away, this place is perennially packed with locals devouring giant shrimps, tuna steaks cooked in walnut leaves and risotto *di mare*. Presentation is often inventive, such as rockfish nuggets wrapped in faux newspaper, and the cellar is stocked with an impressive selection of wines and fizz. *Via del Proconsolo 16, T 055 240 618, www.fishinglab.it*

Osteria dell'Enoteca

The team behind the excellent Enoteca Pitti Gola e Cantina (T 055 212 704) set up here in 2017. It was once an ironworker's, and little has changed from its previous incarnation as Santo Graal – the launch pad for rising star Simone Cipriani (see p042) – with exposed brickwork, artisan furniture and Inox lighting. But chef Nicola Chiappi has introduced a more Tuscan-focused menu, such as tomato gazpacho, *baccalà* mousse, rabbit with homemade pasta, grilled rooster, cuttlefish stew and a thumping great *bistecca alla fiorentina* encircled by roast potatoes. It goes well with a glass of Bucciarelli Chianti Classico, an earthy, dry number with hints of cherry. Conclude proceedings with the homemade *digestivo* of vanilla-infused arancello.
Via Romana 70, T 055 228 6018,
www.osteriadellenoteca.com

Il Santo Bevitore

You could happily spend the entire day in the three San Frediano outlets of Il Santo Bevitore, tucking into breakfast brioches at the vaulted S Forno (T 055 239 8580) before a lunch of *baccalà mantecato* or meatballs at Il Santino (T 055 230 2820) two minutes up the road. Between the two, this trattoria-style bottle-bedecked space draws long queues at the weekend. This is due in no small part to chef Luca Marin's creative Tuscan dishes, such as gazpacho *verde*; risotto with truffles; roasted pigeon with artichoke, foie gras, radish and tangerine; and wild boar with plums, caramelised onions and white asparagus. There are 150 wines on offer. We'd suggest the Baron Ugo 2011 chianti riserva or the Rosso di Valtellina 2014.
Via di Santo Spirito 64-66, T 055 211 264, www.ilsantobevitore.com

IO Osteria Personale

Launching in 2010 with a gutsy 'no pasta' policy and a freeform approach in which diners were invited to compile their own tasting menus, restaurateur Matteo Fantini has since relented, and added gluten-free and veggie options. Now, placing emphasis on seasonality, the likes of tagliatelle with prawns and porcini mushrooms; roasted octopus with chickpea cream, cumin, lime and mint; and wild-fennel ice cream with licorice meringue shine in a more regular format. The wine list leans heavily towards Piemonte, Alto Adige and Tuscany, and also introduces small producers from France, Germany, Austria and Slovenia. The slick interiors, devised together with Studio A Architetti, are defined by bespoke wooden furniture and rustic whitewashed walls.
Borgo San Frediano 167, T 055 933 1341, www.io-osteriapersonale.it

Locale

If your ideal dining ambience is a medieval banquet, the former home of 16th-century diplomat Bartolomeo Concini can provide the setting. Architect Riccardo Musmeci and designer Wainer Barbati ensured that many vestiges of the palace remain in the ground-floor dining rooms – check out the ceiling frescoes and terracotta stove. The basement takes you back a further 300 years, into a labyrinth of shadowy vaulted chambers with long wooden tables, high-backed chairs, hanging copper pans and sputtering candelabra. The cooking is bang up to date, though, as Danilo D'Alessandro reworks Tuscan staples such as Chianina steak, suckling pig and sea bream ravioli. Or just drop by for a French 75 from the zinc bar in the covered courtyard (above). *Via delle Seggiole 12, T 055 906 7188, www.localefirenze.it*

INSIDER'S GUIDE

JONATHAN CALUGI, VISUAL ARTIST

The work of illustrator Jonathan Calugi, created in his studio in Pistoia, is in demand globally. He spends a lot of time in Florence. 'It's flooded with tourists and crushed by history, yet you can still discover authentic places,' he insists. He likes to start the day at Pank La Bulangeria (T 055 239 9798) in Mercato Centrale (see p095). Then he might explore the secondhand bookshops around Via dei Servi, trying to track down tomes from legendary Florentine graphic arts publisher Fondazione Il Bisonte: 'The colours are still so true, bold and intense.' Come lunchtime, a steaming plate of *trippa alla fiorentina* and a glass of chianti is his regular order at Tre Merli (Via dei Fossi 12, T 055 287 062). Afterwards, he often pops into Museo Marino Marini (Piazza San Pancrazio, T 055 219 432) to find inspiration in 'the movement' of the sculptures.

At aperitivo hour, Calugi recommends a Bloody Mary at Gesto (Borgo San Frediano 27, T 055 241 288), before heading to below-the-radar seafood restaurant Lo Skipper (Via degli Alfani 78, T 055 284 019): 'It's like dining on a boat.' He also suggests the Tuscan dishes at trattoria La Burrasca (Via Panicale 6, T 055 215 827) and Vietnamese fare at Com Saigon (Via dell'Agnolo 93, T 055 263 8648), which is renowned for its mushroom-filled steamed rice cakes. If he's having a big night out, he makes a beeline for Circolo Aurora (Piazza Tasso 1/1, T 055 224 059), a joint jumping with live bands.

For full addresses, see Resources.

ART AND DESIGN

GALLERIES, STUDIOS AND PUBLIC SPACES

Renaissance treasures hog the limelight in this city, and rightly so. But a contemporary scene is increasingly emerging from this huge classical shadow. The trailblazing gallery was Poggiali (opposite) but in terms of a local awakening, Base Progetti (see p062) has long been the reference point for conceptual art. As interest grew, Aria (see p068) and Eduardo Secci (see p063) launched in 2009, and early protagonist Gentili (see p070) returned after a hiatus in 2016 in a show of confidence. Now, Florence is full of individual talent too, in particular installation artist Marco Bagnoli, sculptor Daniela De Lorenzo, painter Massimo Barzagli and mixed-media star Letizia Renzini, while performance artist Luigi Presicce lives here. As for the institutions, director Arturo Galansino has dragged Palazzo Strozzi (see p064) into the 21st century, while the council is promoting projects like Ytalia, which scattered 100 site-specific installations by 12 prominent Italians throughout the urban area.

The craft traditions of goldsmithing, iron forging, wood carving, masonry and leatherworking still form the inspiration in design. Studio Lievito (www.studiolievito.com) drew on artisan methods for its geometrical kitchen utensils in marble and stainless steel, and Duccio Maria Gambi (see p058) is an avant-garde master of stone and concrete. And up the road in Prato (see p099), Lottozero (Via Arno 10, T 340 278 7854) is an incubator and exhibitor of textile art. *For full addresses, see Resources.*

Galleria Poggiali

A forerunner of the contemporary scene in Florence, Alessandro Poggiali launched his first gallery back in 1984. It remains one of the standouts in many ways. Even the facade eschews this city's ubiquitous wooden *portone* and cast-iron grilles in favour of a modern concrete-and-glass look. This approach infuses the entire operation, which Poggiali now runs with his two sons, Marco and Lorenzo. They champion a select coterie of established artists, such as Brit John Isaacs (*Yesterday, Today, Tomorrow*, bronze on floor, in the group show 'Faith & Fathom', above), many of whom are Italian, including Manfredi Beninati and Marco Fantini, and sculptor Fabio Viale, in multiple collaborations. There's a sister gallery in Via Benedetta.
Via della Scala 35a, T 055 287 748,
www.galleriapoggiali.com

Atelier Duccio Maria Gambi

After a decade spent in Milan, Rotterdam and Paris, furniture and interior designer Duccio Maria Gambi returned to his native Florence in 2016 to set up his atelier. He studied architectural engineering, and his style has an obvious structural element. It is evident in his 'Meccanico Archeologico' stool, a patchwork of sandstone, porcelain and marble, which was a collaboration with manufacturer Il Casone and London gallery Seeds, and in his 'Petrografico' table, a slab of Luserna stone cut into graphic sections with the incisions painted in enamel. The 'Isometrico' coffee table (above) for Nero in Arezzo is further illustration of Gambi's material-led approach. It is the first in an ongoing series. The asymmetric ensemble of concrete monoliths is beautiful in its simplicity. Visit his studio by appointment. *www.ducciomariagambi.com*

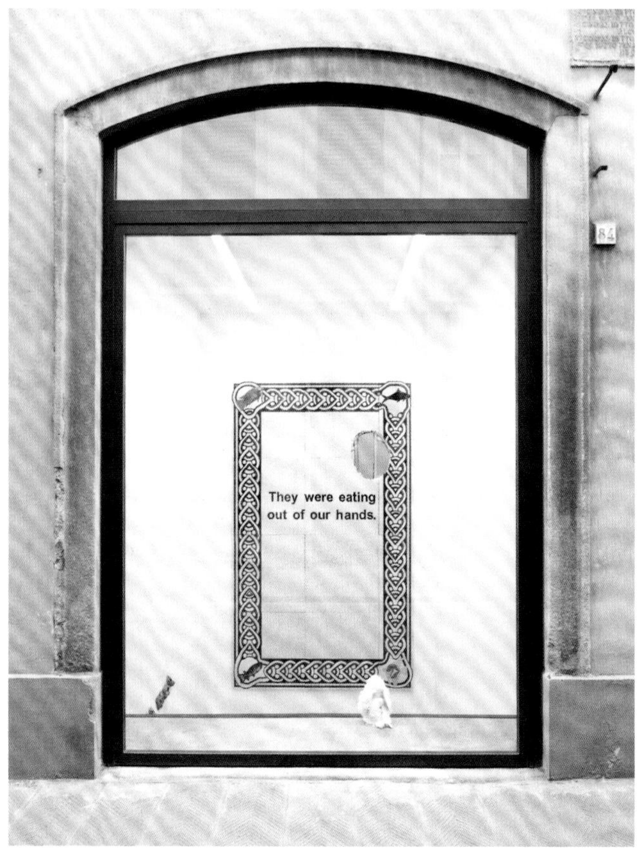

84
They were eating
out of our hands.

Veda

Avant-garde whippersnapper to Galleria Gentili (see p070) across the courtyard, Veda was launched in 2016 by Gianluca Gentili. You can't actually enter the triple-height void, which extends below ground level, but can view the installations around the clock through the glass facade onto the street. Emerging international artists are commissioned to interpret these 30 sq m in four experimental shows per year. New Yorker Hayley Silverman's *The Living Watch Over The Living* fused Biblical imagery and big data, while Norwegian Marius Engh's *Eschscholzia Californica* comprised a single potted tree. Londoner Emily Jones' *Half-Earth* (above) was inspired by EO Wilson's book – a radical proposition to preserve biodiversity. The office is located behind. *Borgo Pinti 84, T 055 906 0519, www.spazioveda.it*

Numeroventi

Martino di Napoli Rampolla's family bought this quarter of the 1510 Palazzo Galli Tassi in 1832. Since taking it over in 2016, he has transformed the 16 rooms into an artistic hub. Frescoes, ancient statues and *pietra serena* remain, but the 5m-high walls of exhibition spaces are now painted white, and other areas have been converted into studios, a shared office and apartments. Numeroventi runs rolling residencies and looks to encourage creative inspiration through collaboration – past participants have included Colombian product designer Natalia Criado, British musician Dev Hynes and local talent Anna Rose ('Atlas', above). Work is shown weekly, and natural wine tastings, launches and other events (check the schedule online) attract the in-crowd.
Via de Pandolfini 20, T 338 245 0055, www.numeroventi.it

Base Progetti Per l'Arte

A collective of 11 artists recognised in their own right founded Base Progetti as a not-for-profit gallery in 1998. Local cofounder Maurizio Nannucci is a seminal figure in Italy's conceptual scene – he has a piece in Museo Novecento (see p025) – while fellow protagonist Vittorio Cavallini is well-known globally. The venue consists of two tiny linked rooms and specialises in site-specific installations in up to 10 shows a year by international names, the likes of which are rarely recognised elsewhere in Florence. Past exhibitions have included François Morellet's 'Noendneon' (above), while Brit land artist Richard Long applied mud to the walls in circular patterns for 'Arno Avon'. Lights are kept on at night so there's something to see around the clock. *Via San Niccolò 18, T 328 962 7778, www.baseitaly.org*

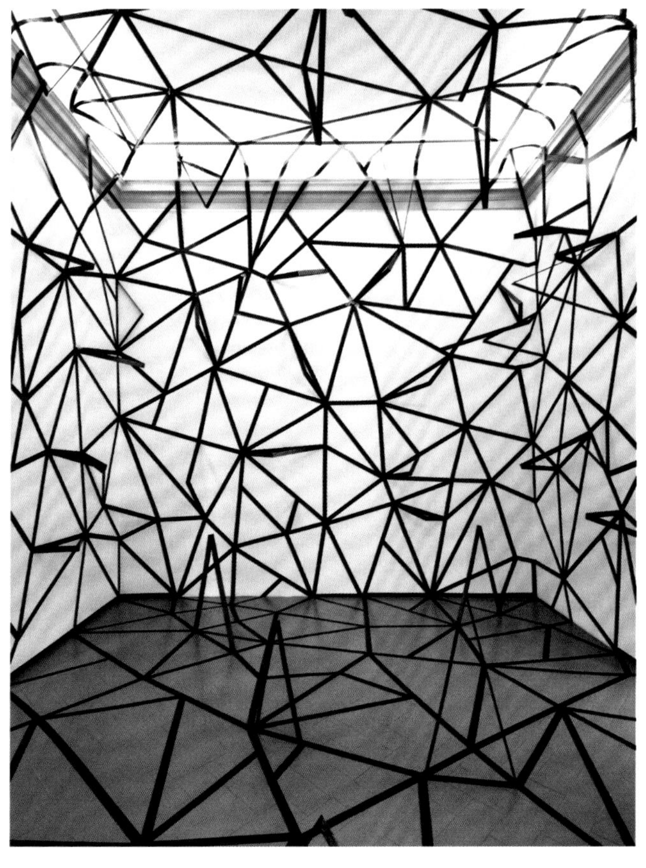

Eduardo Secci

Italy's youngest gallerista when he started in 2009 aged 19, Eduardo Secci has moved his premises around town twice already and now resides in four apartment-style rooms (one with an original ceiling fresco) on the ground floor of the 14th-century Palazzo Ricasoli. His focus is on ambitious installations, often almost architectural in scale, by emerging and mid-career global artists. This is best encapsulated by the 'Tensioni Strutturali' series. 'No 1' featured Esther Stocker's *Senza Titolo* (above) and work by Carlo Bernardini, Monika Grzymala and Roberto Pugliese. Highlights of later editions have been Baptiste Debombourg's cataclysmic cascades in lacquered wood and fragmented glass, and the whirring acoustic sculptures of Bern-based Zimoun.
Piazza Goldoni 2, T 055 661 356,
www.eduardosecci.com

CCC Strozzina

The formidable Palazzo Strozzi dates back to 1538. It was reincarnated in 2007 as a public arts space that hosts themed and interdisciplinary exhibitions. For instance, Liu Xiaodong mixed reportage and painting to study Chinese immigration in the region, and 'Radical Utopias: Beyond Architecture, Florence 1966-1976' (above, bags by Remo Buti and clothing by Lucia Bartolini) delved into a period of extraordinary creativity in the city. Household names such as Damien Hirst and Gerhard Richter keep the visitor numbers up, while homegrown artists are cultivated via an Emerging Talents Award. The Renaissance courtyard, and often the facade of the building, act as backdrops for large-scale site-specific works, such as Wang Yu Yang's *Artificial Moon*.
Palazzo Strozzi, Piazza Strozzi,
T 055 264 5155, www.strozzina.org

Flair

Franco Mariotti and Alessandra Tabacchi's showroom is a moody, masculine, palatial lair. For two decades they've championed vintage and midcentury furniture, as well as contemporary pieces and own-design originals. A series of rooms display 20th-century gems like a pair of reupholstered 1963 Fratelli Saporiti 'Kiushu' armchairs or a 1960 walnut writing desk, beside more modern decorative items such as Ivano Fabbri's dynamic laser-cut geometric wall art, and Elie Hirsch's swirling 'Ellipses' mobiles. The Flair Edition range includes the 'Ice Connect' marble sideboard, brass 'Screen Brut' and Sputnik-style 'Solar' chandelier ('Our work is becoming more brutalist and sculptural,' says Mariotti). Weekdays, 10am to 1pm and 2pm to 7pm. *Lungarno Corsini 24, T 055 267 0154, www.flair.it*

Giardino di Boboli

These magnificent formal gardens, begun in 1549 by Niccolò Pericoli ('Il Tribolo') and continued by Bartolomeo Ammannati and others, were planted for the Medicis, and offer respite from the heat. Wide avenues lead past towering oaks, hedges, grottos, water features and classical statuary such as Stoldo Lorenzi's showboating *Fontana di Nettuno*, dubbed 'The Fork' by locals. There are also a few modern installations, notably Igor Mitoraj's 1998 cracked bronze face *Tindaro Screpolato* and Kan Yasuda's 2000 marble oval *Secret of the Sky*. In the summer of 2017, *In Ordine Sparso* (above), by Helidon Xhixha appeared. A series of stainless-steel pieces resembling molten mirrors, it proved that Florence can mix contemporary and antique with aplomb.
Piazza Pitti 1, T 055 294 883,
www.uffizi.it/en/boboli-garden

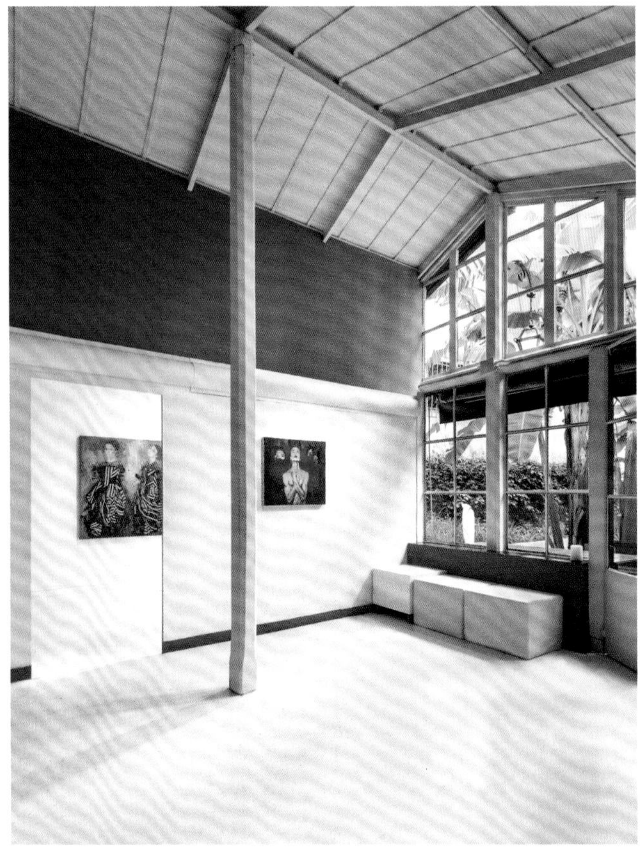

Aria Art Gallery

Since 2009, this bijou gallery, yards from Ponte Vecchio but buffered by the Rosselli del Turco garden, has been the one that the top local artists have been clamouring to impress. Owner Antonio Budetta mainly showcases those who use experimental or ground-breaking techniques. For instance, Fiorentine Michelangelo Bastiani explores a water theme through video projections, installations and holograms; Brescian Angelo Brescianini fires bullets from a gun to create reliefs in stainless steel, often as part of a live performance; and Turk İrfan Önürmen creates psychological portraits from layered tulle. The leitmotif in Bosnian Tarik Berber's 'Toxic Cadmium' paintings (above), which mesh the contemporary with Pompeian frescoes, is the colour red. *Borgo Santi Apostoli 40, T 055 216 150, www.ariaartgallery.com*

Street Levels Gallery

Essentially a single vaulted corridor, this once-abandoned space was reclaimed by a group of young artists and the Progeas Family collective in 2016. A trailblazer in championing urban art in a Renaissance stronghold, the 10 shows per year have featured local tattooist Bue 2530, and Frenopersciacalli, who collaborated on a live VR event in 2017, as well as Romanian Vlad Mititelu, whose 'Ecstacy' paintings (above) mine a graffiti ethos to depict classical bodies and Baroque symbolism. The inaugural exhibition drew attention to 18 Florence-based protagonists, one of whom, the French-born CLET, deploys his impish humour in bastardised signs and large-scale stunts, which have included fixing a huge nose to Torre San Niccolò.
Via Palazzuolo 74, T 339 220 3607,
street-level-gallery.business.site

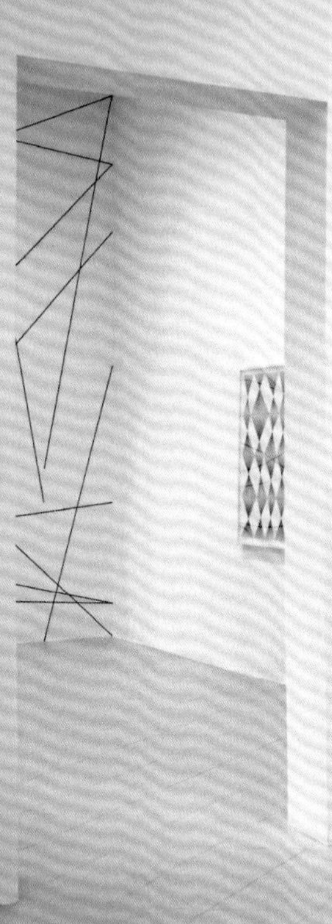

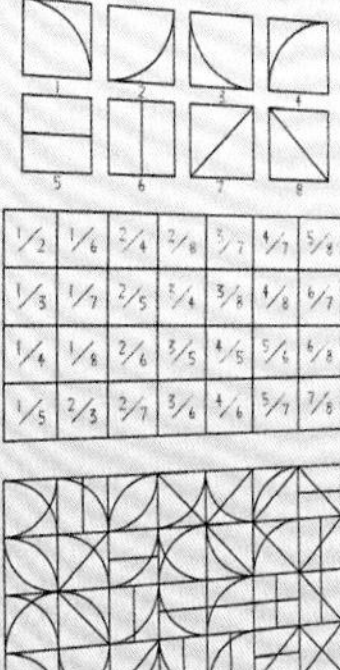
ALL COMBINATIONS OF ARCS FROM CORNERS
AND STRAIGHT LINES IN FOUR DIRECTIONS

Galleria Gentili

Giulietta Innocente relocated her 1991 enterprise to Prato before returning in 2016. She shows established conceptual artists, and represents Italians Luciano Bartolini, Enrico Castellani, Pier Paolo Calzolari and locally based Carlo Guaita. In 'Muro e Parete' (pictured), walls were the canvas for Ignacio Uriarte's paper reliefs and Sol LeWitt's balletic drawings.
Borgo Pinti 80, T 055 906 0519

ARCHITOUR

A GUIDE TO FLORENCE'S ICONIC BUILDINGS

If it's new and more than four inches high, stand by for fireworks. Meddling officials and archaeological finds have stymied even the most inspired proposal, from Arata Isozaki's Uffizi loggia to Foster + Partners' Belfiore station. A clutch of modern structures made it through in the 1930s, mainly propelled by Mussolini's fist, notably Stadio Artemio Franchi (see p013) and Stazione SMN (see p076). Three decades on and interesting development had been banished to the suburbs and the outskirts, from Case Popolari di Sorgane (see p077) to Lando Bartoli's 1961 Sacro Cuore (Via Capo di Mondo 60, T 055 670 148), with its strutted belfry and abstract stained glass, and the sublime Chiesa di San Giovanni Battista (see p074).

However, there's hope for the future, with almost all the action happening in the north-west, on some rare brownfield sites. The Palazzo di Giustizia (see p078) was finally completed in 2009, and Cascine's emerging quarter status was cemented by the unveiling of Maggio Musicale Fiorentino (see p014) in 2011. The extension of the tram network means this area is now only five minutes from SMN. Next up is a multi-use transformation of the 1940 Manifattura Tabacchi, and at last there's real belief that the underground high-speed Belfiore rail link to Bologna will also open here in 2022. Plus ACF Fiorentina may yet get its all-singing, all-dancing stadium (see p013), in a €420m complex to the north in Mercafir, slated for 2021. *For full addresses, see Resources.*

Basilica di Santa Croce

Architecture by Arnolfo di Cambio, frescoes and stained glass by Giotto, Michelangelo's tomb, Donatello's *Annunciation* – it's an impressive list, and this Franciscan church complex, dating from 1294, has as many hits as the Duomo but none of the frenzy. A tour of Vasari's interior and the tombs of the city's luminaries, including Niccolò Machiavelli, should be followed by a quiet wander around the cloister gardens, home to Henry Moore's *Warrior with Shield* and temporary exhibits. The plain Pazzi Chapel, designed by Filippo Brunelleschi but not completed until 14 years after his death in 1460, is a must-see, not least for the shards of light that pierce the dome. Also visit the museum, where you can view Gaddi's *Last Supper* and Orcagna's fragmented fresco. *Piazza Santa Croce 16, T 055 246 6105, www.santacroceopera.it/en*

Chiesa di San Giovanni Battista

Life-affirming, biomorphic and, well, just plain weird – if only more churches looked like this. A 25-minute drive out of the city, hugging the A1 Naples-Milan autostrada, it was built in memory of the 164 workers who died, mainly due to tunnel collapses, in the creation of the motorway network, and completed in 1963. It's a far cry from Giovanni Michelucci's fascist commissions (overleaf) – a markedly organic jostle of pink-and-white stone parabolas punctured by glass strips and a roof of concrete and copper that seems to billow. The sculptures are exquisite, from Pericle Fazzini's bronze carvings at the entrance to Emilio Greco and Venanzo Crocetti's panels of saints, and Giuseppe Pirrone's baptistry doors. Open 9am to 4.30pm (Sunday hours vary). *Campi Bisenzio, A1 Uscita Firenze Nord, T 055 421 9016*

Palazzina Reale di SMN

Giovanni Michelucci's rationalist Stazione Santa Maria Novella opened in 1935, with its own palace to host the royal family on city visits, accessed directly from platform 16. After a restoration, finished in 2015, its marble carapace gleams again, adorned by Italo Griselli's original sculpture *L'Arno e la sua Vallata* (above), the only concession to ornamentation on the facade. However, inside there is wood panelling, parquet flooring, and serpentino verde, Carrara and red Levanto marble. A broad programme of exhibitions, on topics such as regeneration, is open to the public. Enter from the street, via a covered colonnade, or through the station's Reale Firenze bar (T 055 264 5114). In summer, seats are set out around the fountains to form a casual open-air venue. *Piazza della Stazione 50, T 055 015 1600, www.architettifirenze.it*

Casa per Appartamenti

Some 150 'tower houses', built to showcase power and wealth, dominated medieval Florence. Most were destroyed, although Torre dei Rigaletti (Chiasso Cozza) is still standing. Architects Leonardo Savioli and Danilo Santi referenced this legacy in 1967 in their Casa per Appartamenti, which is anchored by a thundering vertical column. It also draws on the modular concept of the metabolist movement, and the interlocking blocks of differing heights form an L-shape that fills a corner plot. The foliage on the terraces, wood shutters and cantilevered ellipsoidal roof soften the austerity of the concrete. For more of Savioli's work, head south-east to Case Popolari di Sorgane (Via Isonzo), a brutalist complex designed from 1957 to 1966, and realised in 1970, to help accommodate a booming population.
Via Piagentina 79

Palazzo di Giustizia

Dubbed by critics the 'monster of Novoli', the civil, criminal and regional courts on the site of the former Fiat plant located to the north-west of the centre have divided opinion like no other building. Proponents applaud the hand of Giovanni Michelucci (see p075) – former teacher to architect Leonardo Ricci – in the integration of civic spheres and people-friendly masterplan. Detractors claim this expensive stone-and-glass jumble of jarring angles, which is the fourth-tallest structure in town, at 72m high, is an unsightly splinter in the skyline. Considering most contemporary projects in Florence are strangled before birth, it's remarkable that Ricci's behemoth rose at all. He first designed it back in the 1970s but the foundation stone was not laid until 2000, six years after he had passed away, and it was inaugurated in 2012. All of which would explain its postmodern vibe.
Viale Alessandro Guidoni 61

SHOPS

THE BEST RETAIL THERAPY AND WHAT TO BUY

Florence's history of craftsmanship and commerce stretches back to the 13th century when the success of the silk, wool and leather trades led to the establishment of powerful guilds of merchants and bankers. Zip forward to the present, and Gucci, Pucci, Cavalli and Ferragamo are Tuscan brands that have conquered the world. The big players congregate along Via de' Tornabuoni and around Piazza della Repubblica. There are plenty of less familiar but no less inspiring local concepts, from Société Anonyme Deux (opposite) to Atelier C (see p086) and Viajiyu (see p089), while Irene Zarrilli showcases emerging designers beside vintage labels at Boutique Nadine (Via de' Benci 32, T 055 247 8274). And the old guard is taking notice too – the 1818 tailor Sartoria Vanni (Via dei Fossi 51, T 055 527 6598) now offers a jetsetting personal service.

The backstreet workshops are still thriving, as artisan techniques have been melded with contemporary ideas. Oltrarno offers rich pickings, in particular the futuro-pastoral hats at Reinhard Plank (Via dei Serragli 34, T 057 157 7809) and totes at Dimitri Villoresi (Via dell'Ardiglione 22, T 366 453 4867). Elsewhere, seek out Bottega delle Antiche Terme (Borgo Santissimi Apostoli 16, T 055 210 552) for handmade shirts, and Michele Chiocciolini (Via del Fico 3, T 055 200 1120) for sculptural bags. If you can only visit one atelier, make it Stefano Bemer (see p082), where shoes are made to last a lifetime.
For full addresses, see Resources.

Société Anonyme Deux

Massimiliano Giannelli's Société Anonyme (T 055 386 0084) shook up the city back in 2006 with a surreal interior inspired by Dadaism and Arte Povera and a tight edit of edgy international fashion labels for men and women. At Société Anonyme Deux, launched in 2016, the focus is on his own label, defined by pieces such as the casual 'Friday' blazer, oversized 'Jap Coat' and voluminous trousers, from the wide-leg, long-crotch 'Indy Short' to the high-waist 'Big Pleats'. You'll also find choice picks from Maison Kitsuné, Ami and McQ. The quirky store, designed with Prato firm Tribeca Factory, features a stripped tree, silver concrete floors, and witty touches such as a meteorite-like changing room, and socks displayed in washing machines. *Via Maggio 60, T 055 530 8428, www.societeanonyme.it*

Stefano Bemer

The late Stefano Bemer founded his gents' cobbler's in 1983, and the legacy continues thanks to Tommaso Melani, who moved the operation to San Niccoló in 2012. Taking centre stage are half a dozen *calzolai*, who will gladly explain the intricacies of skiving and burnishing, through an intoxicating wood-tobacco fug (a result of the leather-making process). Bespoke footwear starts at €2,450, plus an initial outlay of €600 for the last, which will perfectly mirror your instep. The store is festooned with tools of the trade, and the stylish packaging is stacked up on a traditional clay-tile floor. Antique cabinets and wall-mounted boxes display ready-to-wear, which comes in 50 styles including a sneaker, and in a range of textured finishes and bright skins.
Via San Niccolò 2, T 055 046 0476, www.stefanobemer.com

SuperDuper Hats

Tuscans Matteo Gioli and sisters Ilaria and Veronica Cornacchini fuse craftsmanship with modish, innovative concepts – wide-brimmed bowlers with snapbacks, hand-painted trucker caps, and denim turbans for women. All are made by hand, featuring rabbit, hare and beaver felt in winter, and Ecuadorean straw and South-East Asian palm in summer. The unisex 'Goofy Lapin' fedora (above, €310) is fitted with a calf-leather sweatband. Bespoke pieces are made at the atelier in Galluzzo (10km south of the city; by appointment), and an off-the-shelf range is sold at Luisa Via Roma (see p088). The trio also collaborate with fashion collective Art Comes First, and launched a clothing line, Hatters Crew, in 2016. Find more original headwear, and shoes, at Reinhard Plank (see p080).
www.superduperhats.com

Bjørk

Named after the birch tree, conjuring up a Scandi sensibility, concept store Bjørk, run by the cosmopolitan Filippo Anzalone, offers an alternative style that you often struggle to find in this conservative city. Fashion, for both sexes, includes menswear designed by locals Federico Curradi and Lucio Vanotti, alongside lesser-known European labels such as A Kind of Guise and Our Legacy. Also on sale are books and periodicals, art prints and accessories like Nasire's calf-leather laptop case, and 'T525' tote in brilliant blue, and whimsical bronze and brass jewellery by Florence-based Mikinora. The place has a DIY vibe, due to a rather rickety-looking mezzanine level, and the plywood display units and boards, with potted plants dotted about. *Via dello Sprone 25, T 333 979 5939, www.bjorkflorence.com*

Atelier C

This gallery-like emporium opened in 2016 as the creative playground of fashionista Marco Contiello and interiors guru Alice Caporali. She designed almost everything here, from the brass shelving to the oak panelling, inlaid marble tables and marine-blue velvet sofa (all of which can be crafted to order by local artisans). Contiello hand-makes a select range of womenswear with classic silhouettes – dresses in floaty silk and cashmere tops – and also offers haute couture. The handbags, in crocodile skin, calfskin or nubuck leather, are another calling card; bespoke takes two months, or buy off the peg. We were won over by the *scagliola* (a traditional woodworking technique) cigar and jewellery boxes; also on sale are pretty crystal vases. Apart from the textured oxidised artworks courtesy of Bencini Barcelona, all is made in Florence.
Via dei Fossi 33, T 055 289 787, www.ateliercfirenze.it

Luisa Via Roma

The city's fashion trailblazer embraced mindfulness in 2016 with the unveiling of a frond-filled terrace retreat created by Patricia Urquiola, with furniture by Kettal and Moroso. Elsewhere across the three floors, designed by local studio Claudio Nardi, concrete, plexiglass and high-tech prevail, and garments are summoned via tablet, to try on or send home. The ready-to-wear selection is tight, with standouts from Florentine brands including pop icon handbags by Les Petits Joueurs, silk satin kimonos from Caftanii, and Micoli's nappa leather totes. The digital window display showcases artists such as Antoni Tudisco, whose 2017 *Step into the Surreal* stopped traffic. Also check out sister store Luisa Via Roma Contemporary (T 055 217 826).
Via Roma 19-21, T 055 906 4116, www.luisaviaroma.com

Viajiyu

Nicole Still established Viajiyu (a mash-up of '*via*', Italian for road, and '*jiyu*', Japanese for freedom) in 2013 to offer bespoke flats to 'trailblazing' entrepreneurial women. Personal service is key, and Still, born in Ohio and a regular traveller, works here at weekends, ready with an espresso or glass of prosecco. Consultations take 40 minutes (or you can set up a virtual appointment, as well as design your own online). Choose from goatskin, calfskin, velvet or sailcloth, in a vast range of hues, or go for a metallic finish, and customise further with trims, tassels, studs and bows. Handcrafted by local artisans, each pair takes up to eight weeks to make. The mostly white boutique pops with the punchy, bright colours of the fabric swatches, and the shoes themselves.
Borgo Santissimi Apostoli 45, T 055 290 380, www.viajiyu.com

V y T
Santa Marghe

Vyta Santa Margherita

In a one-time first-class waiting room in Giovanni Michelucci's 1930s rail station (see p076), this elegant bar and bakery was converted by Rome firm Colli Daniela Architetto in 2016. It is a highly polished assemblage of pink-hued copper, teal and Verde Alpi marble floors, with 'Pentagon Pendant' lighting by Afroditi Krassa and a filigree screen to separate the counter from a more secluded area furnished with 'Miunn' stools by Lapalma. Mounted on the original boiserie, the black-and-white photos of Venice, San Gimignano and Pisa add to the noirish atmosphere. Drop by to sample the mini *tulipano* muffins, or for a *sfogliatella* and an espresso from the Cimbali coffee machine. In the mall below, at Vyta Fine Food, pick up all manner of packaged Tuscan products, deli items and wine – we would recommend a bottle of Sassoregale's spicy Maremma Toscana.
SMN station, T 06 4778 6878, www.vyta.it

Farmaceutica di Santa Maria Novella

Adjoining the Santa Maria Novella church and looking out over garden cloisters, this pharmacy was opened by Dominican friars in 1612. It marked its fourth centenary with a complete restoration, and the launch of new products such as Acqua di Colonia Lana, a fragrance with accents of cedar, sandalwood, leather, vetiver, musk and rose. The interior is breathtaking, with its 17th-century wood-and-glass cabinets, huge chandeliers and frescoes – the most spectacular in the former sacristy of the Chapel of San Niccolò, painted by Mariotto di Nardo between 1385 and 1405. Look out for ancient remedies such as Acqua di Santa Maria Novella, invented in 1614 to combat hysteria, and Aceto Aromatico, which is said to protect against the plague. *Via della Scala 16, T 055 216 276, www.smnovella.it*

Officina del Poggio

US-born Allison Nicole Hoeltzel launched her bag label in 2013. It's based in Bologna but manufactured in the Florence region, tapping into the rich artisan tradition. The signature 'Safari' range was inspired by a binoculars case, and comes in restrained hues such as marine and tobacco, finished with gold-plated buckles. They are created by a family outfit who process vachetta leather by hand, from layering materials on a mould to create the robust form, to the cutting and stitching. New materials are offered each season – the 2017 velvet version (above, €645) exudes 1970s glam. Order bespoke via the website, choosing crocodile or snakeskin, and lining options and monogramming. Larger models like the circular 'Tamburo' and 'Buckle Tote' are made in the city's western suburbs. *www.officinadelpoggio.com*

Procacci

Saverio Innocenti's makeover has added a more sophisticated aperitivo-friendly vibe to this classic truffle emporium, run by the Antinori family (see p100) for the past two decades. There are now bespoke lamps, zinc tables and tones of grey, but otherwise the 1885 gourmet bottega, with its mosaic-tiled floor, remains gloriously untroubled by the passage of time. The first thing that hits you is the pungent aroma. The second is the genteel ambience. Locals still gather to sample *panini tartufati* (tiny white rolls filled with truffle cream), available to take away, and the walnut shelves are stacked with pâtés, honey and jam. Pop by and pick up one of the specialities such as anchovies in truffle oil or white truffle spread, and a bottle of Marchese Antinori Cuvée Royale. *Via de' Tornabuoni 64, T 055 211 656, www.procacci1885.it*

Mercato Centrale

Archea Associati's intervention revamped the upper floor of Giovanni Mengoni's vast 1874 market, softening the majestic cast-iron frame with huge wicker lampshades and tactile materials such as terracotta, rope and wood. Meanwhile, designer and illustrator Jonathan Calugi (see p054) gave it a coherence with clever branding for the relaunch in 2014. The result is a bustling 'covered city square' that seats 500. On offer are all manner of culinary delights, from skewers of giant prawns to Tuscan classics such as *lampredotto*, made from the fourth stomach of a cow, as well as food and craft beer tastings, and live gigs, be it jazz or gypsy. Pick up a plummy red from L'Enoteca, and a sweet treat at Il Cioccolato e Il Gelato. Open until midnight. *Piazza del Mercato Centrale, T 055 210 214, www.mercatocentrale.it*

ESCAPES

WHERE TO GO IF YOU WANT TO LEAVE TOWN

Tuscany's rolling hills have the power to revive the most frazzled visitor. The challenge is deciding where to go: the wine-producing heartlands of Chianti, the medieval hill towns of the south, the dense chestnut groves of Val d'Orcia, or the long sandy beaches of the Maremma, abutting the azure Tyrrhenian Sea. The secret is to hole up in a bijou retreat and explore at your leisure. Fattoria San Martino (Via Martiena 3, Montepulciano, T 057 871 7463) pushes the organic envelope, while oenophiles should head to the restored 16th-century Villa Bordoni (Via San Cresci 31-32, Mezzuola, T 055 854 6230), on a hill among vineyards. Villa Lena (Strada Comunale di Toiano 42, Palaia, T 058 708 3111) is an *agriturismo* set in olive groves, with an artists-in-residence programme, truffle hunts and pasta-making sessions. Or go grander, at Rosewood Castiglion del Bosco (T 057 7191 3001), a gorgeous estate within Val d'Orcia.

For culture, Fattoria di Celle (Via Montalese, Santomato, T 057 347 9907) has an extraordinary collection of sculpture by Giuseppe Penone, Alberto Burri, Robert Morris et al, dotted among the follies in a stately park (book a tour in advance). And fans of biomorphic architecture should head towards Piombino on the coast to see Vittorio Giorgini's outlandish creations. Check out the 1957 Casa Esagono, a beehive on stilts in the woods, and 1962 Casa Saldarini, which evokes some kind of snaking antediluvian beast.

For full addresses, see Resources.

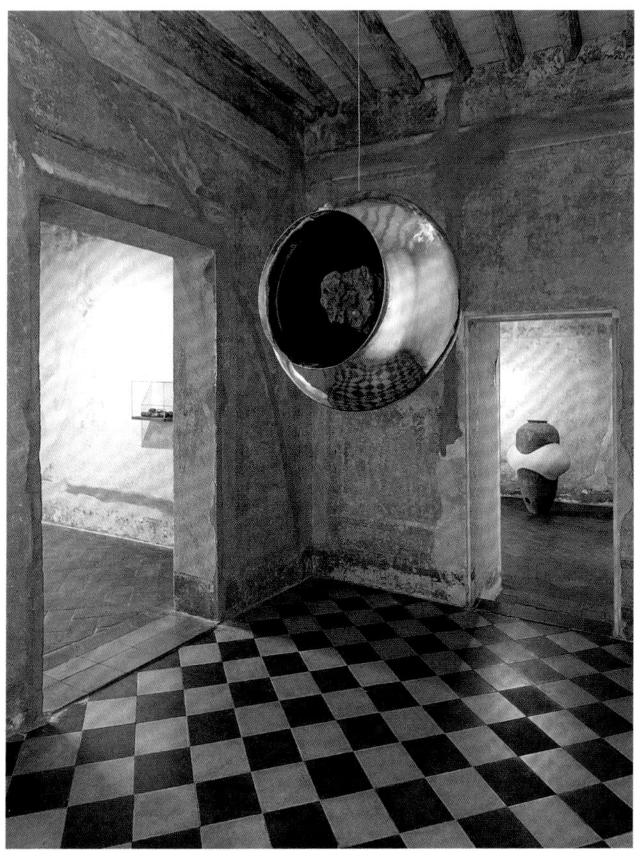

Galleria Continua, San Gimignano

It's worth enduring the coach-party hell of hilltop village Sam Gimignano – its famed towers were an exercise in one-upmanship between the *nobili* in the 12th and 13th centuries – to seek out the contemporary art gallery Continua. Established in 1990, it showcases global names, such as Anish Kapoor and Antony Gormley, as well as the less well-known, like Kosovan conceptual artist Sislej Xhafa. It is the brainchild of three local friends, who went on to open sister outposts in France, China and Cuba, but never forgot their roots. Drop in at the Michelin-starred Cum Quibus (T 057 794 3199) for innovative Tuscan fare – try the signature *mezzovo* (egg yolk with sheep-cheese mousse and truffle). San Gimignano is an hour's drive south-west of Florence.
Via del Castello 11, T 057 794 3134, www.galleriacontinua.com

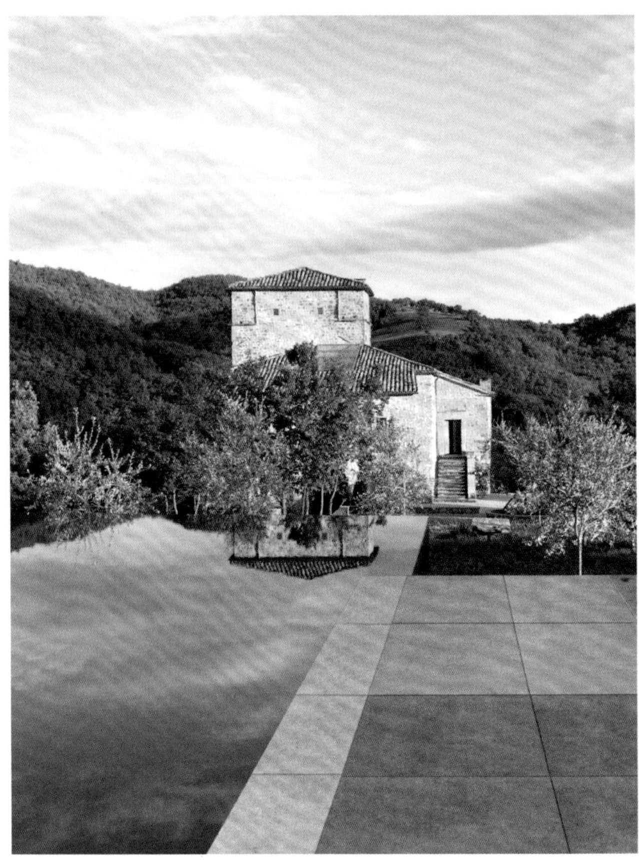

Torre di Moravola, Umbria

Architect Christopher Chong and artist/designer Seonaid Mackenzie discovered this abandoned 12th-century tower, in Umbria, roughly two hours' drive from Florence, in 1999. Nine years and 1,500 drawings later, they had transformed it into a miracle of medieval modernism, with seven suites featuring grey *pietra serena* floors, concealed lighting and a few choice antiques. Chong's minimal sensibilities are responsible for the folded-steel floating stairs, which link the rooms, the pared-down dining area and the 25m infinity pool (above), from which you can enjoy views over rolling hills. It is not the easiest place to find, but switch off your sat nav and ease your way into a slower, lo-tech age, using brainpower and a map.
Montone, T 075 946 0965, www.moravola.com

Centro Pecci Arte Contemporanea

Just outside Florence (20 minutes from SMN station), Prato is historically known for its textile manufacturing. However, its Centro Pecci was given a new lease of life in 2016 with the renovation of rationalist architect Italo Gamberini's original 1988 building. It's now wrapped in Maurice Nio's futuristic semicircular bronze-coloured metallic extension (above), whose wispy tower evokes an antenna. Inside are more than 1,000 works spanning 70 years, the core from collections amassed by locals, notably the Beccaglia family, Carlo Palli and Alessandro Grassi, with a haul of Arte Povera and the Transavantgarde, as well as sound sculpture, architectural drawings, concrete poetry and artists' films. The temporary shows are equally fascinating.
Viale della Repubblica 277, T 0574 5317, www.centropecci.it

Antinori nel Chianti Classico

It is well worth the 30-minute trip to the Antinori winery – a study in architectural stealth completed in 2013. Florence firms Archea Associati and Hydea collaborated around the aim of invisibility to landscape and recess most of this huge complex into the bucolic hillside, which they opened up with circular apertures in order to feed light below. The lower terrace comprises offices, an auditorium, a museum and a cavernous cellar, clad in terracotta and punctuated by dramatically cantilevered glass-walled tasting rooms (opposite). An exterior weathered-steel staircase (above) corkscrews up to an expansive overhanging roof, and restaurant Rinuccio 1180 (T 055 235 9720). Pick up a case of Villa Antinori Chianti Classico Riserva – a Sangiovese blend bursting with fruit and spicy notes. *Via Cassia per Siena 133, San Casciano in Val di Pesa, T 055 235 9700, www.antinorichianticlassico.it*

Museo dei Bozzetti, Pietrasanta

At the foot of the marble-rich Apuan Alps, 90 minutes from Florence, Pietrasanta has drawn sculptors since the 14th century, and the medieval town is peppered with foundries, studios and galleries. Museo dei Bozzetti opened in 1984 in the former convent of Sant'Agostino, and provides an invaluable insight into the creative process of almost 350 artists. However, the real draw is the 60 or so public works that are dispersed through the streets, gardens and squares as part of the Contemporary Sculpture Park project. You'll come across large-scale pieces by Igor Mitoraj, Giuliano Vangi, Giò Pomodoro, Kan Yasuda, Stefano Pierotti and Jiménez Deredia, whose 2005 *Continuación* (above) sits appropriately on a roundabout. Check online for the full list.
Via Sant'Agostino 1, T 058 479 5500, www.museodeibozzetti.it

Monteverdi Tuscany Hotel

Two hours' drive south out of the city, past rolling hills, vineyards and poplars, you'll find this 17-room hotel and accompanying villas threaded throughout the ancient hamlet of Castiglioncello del Trinoro. The suites, Giancarla Bodoni's restaurant, an enoteca (hosting sunset wine tastings) and a spa occupy separate buildings, restored by owner Michael Cioffi and designer Ilaria Miani employing traditional techniques, and in collaboration with landscape expert Enzo Margheriti. Artists and musicians are invited to reside here for extended periods in return for exhibiting their works in the gallery or performing chamber concerts in the 14th-century Chiesa di Sant'Andrea, and scientists from the university in Siena oversee a private archaeological dig.
Via di Mezzo, T 057 826 8146, www.monteverdituscany.com

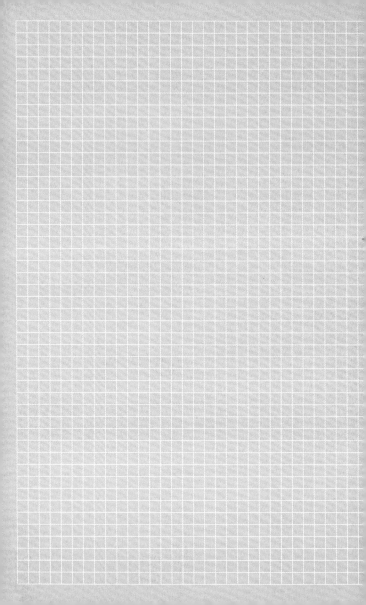

NOTES

SKETCHES AND MEMOS

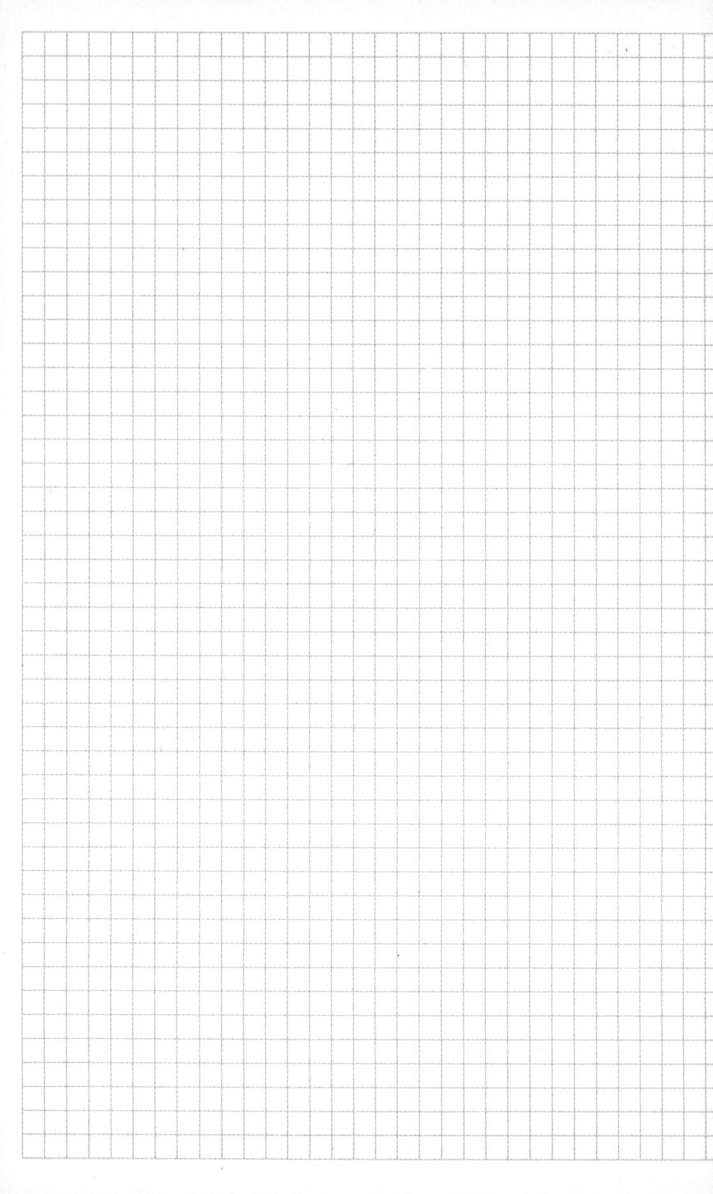

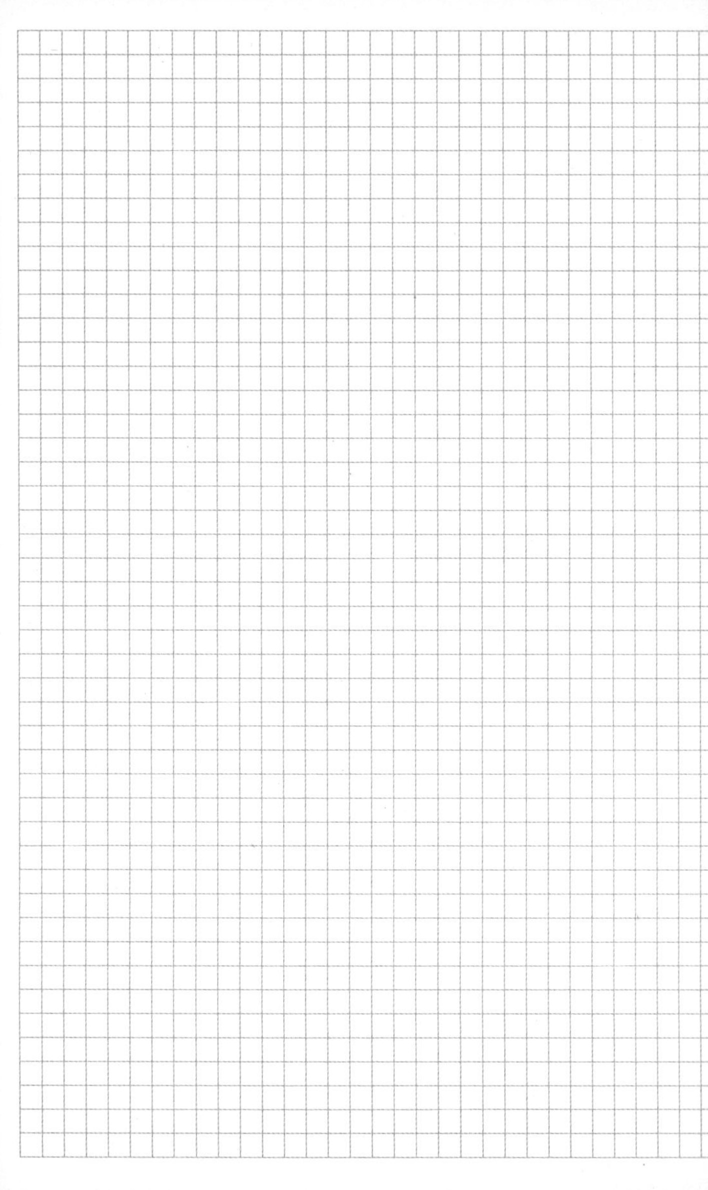

RESOURCES

CITY GUIDE DIRECTORY

A

Antinori nel Chianti Classico 100
Via Cassia per Siena 133
San Casciano in Val di Pesa
T 055 235 9700
www.antinorichianticlassico.it

Aria Art Gallery 068
Borgo Santi Apostoli 40
T 055 216 150
www.ariaartgallery.com

Atelier C 086
Via dei Fossi 33
T 055 289 787
www.ateliercfirenze.it

Atelier Duccio Maria Gambi 058
www.ducciomariagambi.com

B

Base Progetti Per l'Arte 062
Via San Niccolò 18
T 328 962 7778
www.baseitaly.org

Basilica di San Lorenzo 009
Piazza San Lorenzo 9
T 055 216 634

Basilica di Santa Croce 073
Piazza Santa Croce 16
T 055 246 6105
www.santacroceopera.it/en

Bjørk 085
Via dello Sprone 25
T 333 979 5939
www.bjorkflorence.com

Bottega delle Antiche Terme 080
Borgo Santissimi Apostoli 16
T 055 210 552

Boutique Nadine 080
Via de' Benci 32
T 055 247 8274
www.boutiquenadine.it

Buca Lapi 032
Via del Trebbio 1
T 055 213 768
www.bucalapi.com

Buonerìa 014
Via del Fosso Macinante 4
T 055 365 500
www.buoneria.com

La Burrasca 054
Via Panicale 6
T 055 215 827

C

Cantinetta Antinori 032
Piazza Antinori 3
T 055 292 234
www.cantinetta-antinori.com

Casa Esagono 096
Piombino
www.archiviovittoriogiorgini.it

Casa per Appartamenti 077
Via Piagentina 79

Case Popolari di Sorgane 077
Via Isonzo

CCC Strozzina 064
Palazzo Strozzi
Piazza Strozzi
T 055 264 5155
www.strozzina.org

Centro Pecci Arte Contemporanea 099
Viale della Repubblica 277
Prato
T 0574 5317
www.centropecci.it

Chiesa di San Giovanni Battista 074
Campi Bisenzio
A1 Uscita Firenze Nord
T 055 421 9016

O

Ora d'Aria 039
Via dei Georgofili 11
T 055 200 1699
www.oradariaristorante.com

Osteria dell'Enoteca 050
Via Romana 70
T 055 228 6018
www.osteriadellenoteca.com

Osteria di Passignano 039
Via Passignano 33
T 055 807 1278
www.osteriadipassignano.com/en

P

Palazzina Reale di SMN 076
Piazza della Stazione 50

Palazzo di Giustizia 078
Viale Alessandro Guidoni 61

Palazzo Medici Riccardi 009
Via Camillo Cavour 3

Palazzo Pitti 009
Piazza Pitti 1
T 055 294 883
www.uffizi.it/palazzo-pitti

Palazzo Vecchio 012
Piazza della Signoria
T 055 276 8325
www.museicivicifiorentini.comune.fi.it/en/palazzovecchio

Pank La Bulangeria 054
Mercato Centrale
T 055 239 9798

Pampaloni 033
Via del Gelsomino 99
T 347 514 5468
restaurant.pampaloni.com

Panificio Elleci 035
Via Giuseppe la Farina 22
T 055 242 811

Procacci 094
Via de' Tornabuoni 64
T 055 211 656
www.procacci1885.it

R

Rasputin 032
Borgo Tegolaio 21
T 055 280 399

#Raw 034
Via Sant'Agostino 11
T 055 219 379

Reale Firenze 076
Piazza Stazione 1
Via Valfonda
Stazione di Santa Maria Novella
T 055 264 5114
www.realefirenze.it/en

Reinhard Plank 080
Via dei Serragli 34
T 057 157 7809
www.reinhardplank.it/plankshop
Open Tuesday to Saturday, 3.30pm to 7.30pm

Rinuccio 1180 100
Antinori nel Chianti Classico
Via Cassia per Siena 133
San Casciano in Val di Pesa
T 055 235 9720
www.antinorichianticlassico.it

S

Sacro Cuore 072
Via Capo di Mondo 60
T 055 670 148

Il Santino 051
Via di Santo Spirito 60
T 055 230 2820
www.ilsantobevitore.com

HOTELS

ADDRESSES AND ROOM RATES

AdAstra 017
Room rates:
double, from €160
Via del Campuccio 53
T 055 075 0602
www.adastraflorence.it

Casa Schlatter 016
Room rates:
double, from €90
Viale dei Mille 14
T 347 118 0215
www.casaschlatter-florence.com

Fattoria San Martino 096
Room rates:
double, from €190
Via Martiena 3
Montepulciano
T 057 871 7463
www.fattoriasanmartino.it

Firenze Number Nine 016
Room rates:
double, from €170
Via dei Conti 9
T 055 293 777
www.firenzenumbernine.com/en

JK Place 021
Room rates:
double, from €550;
Penthouse, from €1,300
Piazza Santa Maria Novella 7
T 055 264 5181
www.jkplace.com/en

Hotel Lungarno 020
Room rates:
double, from €400
Borgo San Jacopo 14
T 055 2726 4000
www.lungarnocollection.com/hotel-lungarno

Monteverdi Tuscany Hotel 103
Room rates:
double, from €590;
villa, from €1,400
Via di Mezzo
Castiglioncello del Trinoro
T 057 826 8146
www.monteverdituscany.com

Portrait Firenze 020
Room rates:
suite, from €480;
Ponte Vecchio Suite, from €7,000
Lungarno degli Acciaiuoli 4
T 055 2726 8000
www.lungarnocollection.com/portrait-firenze

Relais Santa Croce 016
Room rates:
double, from €200
Via Ghibellina 87
T 055 234 2230
www.baglionihotels.com

Riva Lofts 022
Room rates:
suite, from €190;
Loft Studio, from €330
Via Baccio Bandinelli 98
T 055 713 0272
www.rivalofts.com/en

Rosewood Castiglion del Bosco 096
Room rates:
double, from €930
Località Castiglion del Bosco
Montalcino
T 057 7191 3001
www.rosewoodhotels.com/en/castiglion-del-bosco

Il Salviatino 018
Room rates:
double, from €450;
Affresco Suite, from €1,100
Via del Salviatino 21
T 055 904 1111
www.salviatino.com

Savoy 016
Room rates:
double, from €600
Piazza della Repubblica 7
T 055 27 351
www.roccofortehotels.com

SoprArno Suites 017
Room rates:
double, from €150;
Deluxe 26, from €150
Via Maggio 35
T 055 046 8719
www.soprarnosuites.com/en

Torre di Moravola 098
Room rates:
suite, from €260
Montone
Umbria
T 075 946 0965
www.moravola.com

Le Tre Stanze 016
Room rates:
double, from €120
Via dell'Oriuolo 43
T 329 212 8756
www.letrestanze.it

Villa Bordoni 096
Room rates:
double, from €150
Via San Cresci 31-32
Mezzuola
Greve-in-Chianti
T 055 854 6230
www.villabordoni.com/en

Villa Lena 096
Room rates:
double, from €140
Strada Comunale di Toiano 42
Palaia
T 058 708 3111
www.villa-lena.it/en

WALLPAPER* CITY GUIDES

Executive Editor
Jeremy Case

Author
Jonathan Lee

Photography Editor
Rebecca Moldenhauer

Art Editor
Jade R Arroyo

Editorial Assistant
Charlie Monaghan

Photo Assistant
Daniëlle Siobhán Mol

Sub-editors
Greg Hughes
Julia Newcomb

Contributors
Claudio Meli
Elisa Miglionico
Silvia Fontana
Francesca Pazzagli
Federica Prayer

Intern
Laura Ferguson

Florence Imprint
First published 2009
Third edition 2018

ISBN 978 0 7148 7647 4

More City Guides
www.phaidon.com/travel

Follow us
@wallpaperguides

Contact
wcg@phaidon.com

Original Design
Loran Stosskopf

Map Illustrator
Russell Bell

Production Controller
Gif Jittiwutikarn

Assistant Production Controller
Sarah Scott

Wallpaper* Magazine
161 Marsh Wall
London E14 9AP
contact@wallpaper.com

Editor-in-Chief
Tony Chambers

Wallpaper*® is a registered trademark of Time Inc (UK)

Phaidon Press Limited
Regent's Wharf
All Saints Street
London N1 9PA

Phaidon Press Inc
65 Bleecker Street
New York, NY 10012

All prices and venue information are correct at time of going to press, but are subject to change.

A CIP Catalogue record for this book is available from the British Library.

PHOTOGRAPHERS

A&B Photodesign
Florence city view, inside front cover
Duomo, pp010-011
Stadio Artemio Franchi, p013
Maggio Musicale Fiorentino, pp014-015
SoprArno Suites, p017
Il Salviatino, pp018-019
JK Place, p021
Riva Lofts, p022, p023
La Ménagère, p026, p027
Gurdulù, p031
Pampaloni, p033
#Raw, p034
La Cucina di Pescepane, p035
Foody Farm, p038
Ora d'Aria, p039
Ciblèo Tortelli e Ravioli, pp040-041
Essenziale, p042
Italian Tapas, p043
Gosh, p044, p045
Zeb, p046
Ditta Artigianale, p047
Fishing Lab Alle Murate, pp048-049
Osteria dell'Enoteca, p050
Il Santo Bevitore, p051
IO Osteria Personale, p052
Locale, p053
Jonathan Calugi, p055
Galleria Poggiali, p057
Aria Art Gallery, p068
Street Levels Gallery, p069
Chiesa di San Giovanni Battista, p074, p075
Palazzina Reale di SMN, p076
Casa per Appartamenti, p077
Palazzo di Giustizia, pp078-079
Stefano Bemer, p082, p083
Bjørk, p085
Atelier C, pp086-087
Viajiyu, p089

Oliviero Olivieri
Palazzo Vecchio, p012
Soulspace, p030
Basilica di Santa Croce, p073

Ela Bialkowska, Okno Studio
Galleria Continua, San Gimignano, p097

Carlo Cantini
Base Progetti Per l'Arte, p062

Tommaso Cappelletti
CCC Strozzina, p064

Collidanielarchitetto
Vyta Santa Margherita, pp090-091

Ivan D'Ali
Centro Pecci Arte Contemporanea, p099

Marina Denisova
Numeroventi, p061

Erio Forli
Museo dei Bozzetti, p102

Jacopo Menzani
Galleria Gentili, pp070-071

Deferrai Modesti
Libreria Brac, p036, p037

Pietro Savorelli
Mercato Centrale, p095

FLORENCE

A COLOUR-CODED GUIDE TO THE HOT 'HOODS

SANTA MARIA NOVELLA
Michelucci's station, Mercato Centrale and sophisticated hotels counterpoint the churches

SAN MARCO
Ditch the crowds beelining for the Accademia by touring this area's elegant gardens

CAMPO DI MARTE
Premier sporting facilities are housed near some of the city's best modern architecture

OLTRARNO
South of the Arno you'll find the beating heart of artisanal Florence, and plenty of hip bars

SANTA CROCE
Locals congregate in this district, drawn by the food market and top-notch restaurants

SAN GIOVANNI
It's all here – the major Renaissance sights, the super-brand shops and swarms of tourists

For a full description of each neighbourhood, see the Introduction.
Featured venues are colour-coded, according to the district in which they are located.